THE GREAT SEARCH

If I could introduce you to ten amazing people whose influence could transform your life by energizing your spiritual quest, they would be the nine visionaries featured in The Great Search ... *plus a tenth, the author John Philip Newell himself. What a treasure this book is!*
Brian McLaren, author of *Life After Doom*

In magnificent cadences of measured writing, Newell profiles nine prophets of today's ecological crisis ... Life and death are set before us. Choose life!
Alastair McIntosh, author of *Soil and Soul*

A moving and powerful volume ... This book points us in wise directions.'
Bill McKibben, author of *The End of Nature*

This book sings the songs of a loving heart, expressing the yearnings of the divine within ... His words feel like touchstones, guiding lights in a time of darkness.
Rabbi Nahum Ward-Lev, author of *The Liberating Path of the Hebrew Prophets: Then and Now*

In The Great Search, *John Philip Newell taps into the wisdom of sages spanning time, geography and faiths to quench today's spiritual thirst. Rather than focusing on traditional teaching about God, we are challenged to experience Divine encounters deep within ourselves, through our neighbours and enemies, and, indeed, in all creation.*

In a world where we encounter intolerance, prejudice, the primacy of self-interest at both a personal and national level, and, not least, the degradation of our planet, this is a spiritual search which is as timely as it is necessary.
Lord Wallace of Tankerness

Also by John Philip Newell and published by Wild Goose:

Christ of the Celts
Each Day & Each Night

THE GREAT SEARCH

Turning to Earth and Soul
in the Quest for Healing and Home

John Philip Newell

wild goose publications   www.ionabooks.com

Copyright © John Philip Newell 2024

First published in the UK 2024 by
Wild Goose Publications
Suite 9, Fairfield
1048 Govan Road, Glasgow G51 4XS, Scotland
A division of Iona Community Trading CIC
Limited Company Reg. No. SC156678
www.ionabooks.com

ISBN 978-1-80432-346-5

Cover photo © Martin Brayley | Dreamstime.com

All rights reserved. No part of this publication may be reproduced in any form or by any means, including photocopying or any information storage or retrieval system, without written permission from the publisher via PLSclear.com.

John Philip Newell has asserted his right in accordance with the Copyright, Designs and Patents Act, 1988, to be identified as the author of this work.

Scripture quotations, unless otherwise noted, are taken from the New Revised Standard Version Bible. Copyright © 1989 National Council of the Churches of Christ in the United States of America. Used by permission. All rights reserved worldwide.

Overseas distribution
Australia: Willow Connection Pty Ltd, 1/13 Kell Mather Drive, Lennox Head NSW 2478
New Zealand: Pleroma, Higginson Street, Otane 4170, Central Hawkes Bay

Printed in the UK by Page Bros (Norwich) Ltd

To four wise women
who like pillars of the temple
have stood strong in support these many years
Merle Chambers
Margaret Anne Fohl
Frannie Hall Kieschnick
and
Margaret Woodson Nea

Contents

Introduction   11

PART ONE
1. Seeking Vision: Thomas Berry   23
2. Seeking Earth: Nan Shepherd   41
3. Seeking Presence: Martin Buber   59

PART TWO
4. Seeking Awareness: Carl Jung   79
5. Seeking Wellness: Julian of Norwich   96
6. Seeking Love: Jalaluddin Rumi   112

PART THREE
7. Seeking Wisdom: Rabindranath Tagore   131
8. Seeking Meaning: Etty Hillesum   148
9. Seeking Faith: Edwin Muir   167

Conclusion   185
Appendix: A Nine-Day Cycle of Meditative Practice   193
Acknowledgments   203
Notes   205

Introduction

Search and you will find.
– *Matthew 7:7*

We are living through a time of immense transition as old systems of authority and belief are questioned. A new vision of reality is trying to be born. Earth and humanity need healing. The way we have lived on this planet is unsustainable. And the way our societies are plagued by racism, injustice and violence is wrong. We need change. Religion as we have known it has failed to adequately address the most urgent challenges of humanity, including the threatened plight of Earth. These challenges are not just ecological, and political, and economic. They are also spiritual. That is why there is a quest of soul today for new depths of wisdom to guide us into well-being, both individually and together.

Something new is emerging. We need to listen to the stirrings of the Spirit within us and within the body of Earth, and change. The good news is that our spiritual traditions have changed in the past and can change again. In Christianity, for instance, there was the Great Schism of the eleventh century that reflected the distinctness of East and West in the unfolding life of the church. Or there was the Great Reformation of sixteenth-century Europe that spawned massive protest for change and questioned old hierarchies of domination. Similarly, there was the Great Awakening of eighteenth-century America that gave birth to more personal expressions of faith. Today we are in another era of change, perhaps the most important we have ever faced in the history of our religious inheritance. It can be called the Great Search. We are seeking healing as an Earth community, and we are longing for a new sense of home spiritually. Vast numbers of us have left the four walls of institutional religion. Others are choosing to stay. But whether we remain in the religious traditions of our birth or move beyond them, we need new vision if we are to find healing in our relationship with Earth and one another.

"Seek and you will find," says Jesus. This is the promise at the heart of the Great Search today. And it is the hope that inspires the writing of this book.

Simone Weil, the French philosopher who as a young Jewish woman was forced to flee France after the Nazi occupation of her homeland during World War II, spoke of the "efficacy of desire".[1] By this she meant that getting in touch with the deepest longings of our hearts is essential if we are to see their realization in our lives and world. In other words, it is efficacious. It helps bring about the birth of something new. Our spiritual yearnings are like seeds of new life. To be alert to them together, to name them and nurture them, helps them grow and unfold in ways we may not yet even have imagined.

In this book I am trying to give expression to the yearnings of today for healing and for a new sense of home spiritually in relation to Earth and our true depths, exploring how it is we are to nurture these yearnings of the Spirit and bring them to fullness in our lives and world. I will be doing this by drawing on the teachings of wise figures who have gone before us, channelling their truths into the heart of this moment in time. This transmission of wisdom from the past can help us engage with the challenges confronting us and find what we are most deeply longing for. Our religious traditions have not been strong at encouraging us to get in touch with our deepest longings, but we must do so now if we are to live and act from our true depths for the well-being of Earth and one another.

The Great Search falls into three parts. Part 1 is shaped by the question, "What are we seeking?" The response is threefold. We are seeking expanded vision, true relationship with Earth, and a greater sense of spiritual presence in the relationships and encounters of our lives. Part 2 is guided by the inquiry, "Why are we searching?" We are searching because we need more awareness, more well-being, and more love. And Part 3 is shaped by the question, "How are we to search?" The response is that we do this by accessing the wisdom of many traditions, by looking for meaning in both the joys and sorrows of life, and by reimagining what we mean by faith.

In each part of the book, I draw on the wisdom of three great teachers. Some of them anticipated the Great Search that we are in the middle of today. Others are simply shining light for us from afar, from other moments in time and other parts of the world. Some of them are men, others are women. Some are theologians and spiritual masters, while others are poets or scientists. Some are Christian, and others are Jewish or Hindu or Muslim. But all of them are writers of the soul, offering us spiritual wisdom for this moment in time. Their teachings are like sunlight and water given to feed the seeds of yearning that are germinating deep in the soil of our souls. The wisdom of the past is ours to help shape the future. *The Great Search* is not just a book about ideas. It also sets out to practically tend the longings of our hearts. At the end of each chapter, I provide a simple meditative practice to further deepen our attentiveness to the stirrings of the Spirit within us and within the body of Earth. Then, at the end of the book, I collect these into an appendix to form a nine-day cycle of spiritual practice for ongoing use.

The Great Search is happening in the realm of Christianity and beyond it. And its equivalent is happening in all the great spiritual traditions of humanity. Some of us are searching from within the four walls of our religious inheritance, and others are seeking in new uncharted territory beyond the bounds of tradition. We need one another. For this journey is not simply about the well-being and survival of religion. It is about the well-being and survival of the world. My own path has increasingly taken me outside the church. I will always see myself as a son of the Christian household, gratefully standing in an ancient stream of wisdom that stretches back to Jesus. I have not lost my faith. I am thankful for being rooted in a particular religious tradition. But it was important for me a few years ago to relinquish my ordination as a minister of the church. I did it quietly with no fanfare. And now that I am writing about it, I don't want to overstate it. It was simply a decision I needed to make in response to the urgings of the Spirit in my own soul. I could no longer personally reconcile the formal teachings of the church, shaped by the creeds of fourth-century Imperial Christianity, with the spiritual vision of Earth's sacredness and the sacredness of every human being that I am committed to following in my life and teachings.[2]

The turning point for me came in 2018 during a pilgrimage week on Iona in the Western Isles of Scotland, that little island in the sea that sits like a jewel on the edge of the Atlantic and to which thousands of pilgrims come every year from all over the world in search of new beginnings. I was with my rabbi, Nahum Ward-Lev. I call him mine because he is like a brother to me. When we first met, more than twenty years ago in the high desert of New Mexico, we connected at a deep level. And soon we began to lead retreats together. Early on I overheard him saying to some of our participants, "When John Philip teaches, it comes out Christian, but it goes in Jewish!" Well, that is exactly how I feel about him but in reverse. He is a rabbi who deeply feeds my Christian soul. We are all on the same spiritual journey whichever religious language we are speaking.

Our first full day of pilgrimage together on Iona was a Sunday, and we attended the morning communion service at the Abbey on Iona. I was so pleased to have Nahum and his wife, Shelley, with me on the island, and to be together in one of my favourite churches in the world, the thirteenth-century Iona Abbey, with its mighty red-hued granite walls and its smoothed centuries-worn stone floor. But as I sat through the service that morning, it struck me in a new way that many of the words we typically use in Christian worship, in our creeds and scriptures, as well as in our hymns and prayers, are disrespectful toward other faiths. Often, they are recited and sung by men and women who would not wish to make claims of superiority over other spiritual traditions. Much of it is just the sheer weight of exclusivity in our inherited religious language. The church would be a very different place, I believe, if we all were to sit through a Sunday morning service with someone from another religious tradition whom we love and respect. We would hear it all very differently. I certainly did that Sunday morning on Iona.

At the end of the service, I felt I needed somehow to apologize to Nahum and Shelley. Some of the language that had been used in worship that morning was offensive, not only to *them* but to the people of every other great spiritual tradition in the world. Not quite knowing what to say, I asked them to join me in the abbey cloister so that I could show them a work of art by the Jewish sculptor Jacques Lipchitz, who as a war refugee had escaped Nazi-occupied France to eventually find sanctuary in America.

The sculpture, which Lipchitz called *Our Lady of Delight* (more commonly known as *The Descent of the Spirit*), depicts the Spirit, in the form of a dove, descending onto an abstract divine feminine figure that opens to give birth to a lamb. The sculpture points to the story of the Christ Child, conceived by the Spirit in the womb of Mary, and it points also to the story of Earth, conceived by the Spirit in the womb of the universe. In other words, everything is of God. And everything has been born with the sacred innocence and vulnerability of a lamb. On the back of the sculpture in French are inscribed the artist's words of dedication. In translation they read, "Jacob Lipchitz, Jew, faithful to the tradition of his ancestors, has made this virgin for the goodwill of every human being on Earth so that the Spirit might prevail."

Standing in front of the sculpture that morning with Nahum and Shelley, my intention was to speak words of comfort to them. But when

I tried to speak, I began to weep, and all I could say was, "I am so ashamed." They took me in their arms, and I wept. I had wanted to comfort them. But it was they who comforted me.

In that moment I realized I needed to let go of my ordination as a Christian minister. I was feeling deeply the disconnect between my teachings of the sacredness of Earth and every human being and the foundational creedal statements of Western Christianity. I recognized that it was a big decision to be making, with many hurdles still ahead of me, but I felt relieved to be letting go of the weight of Christianity's centuries of exclusivist teachings about Jesus so that I could focus more simply on the universal wisdom of Jesus for today.

A few months later I was attending the funeral service of a friend in Canada and ended up sitting beside one of my former students, Leed Jackson, a broad spirit who had never been able to accept the restrictions of religious language and practice. After the service we went out for lunch together with another dear friend, and I told them about my decision to relinquish ordination. As Leed listened, tears welled in his eyes. He leaned toward me, placing his hand on my heart, and said, "John Philip, you're doing this for me and for the many like me who are in spiritual exile today."

I hadn't, in fact, been thinking about Leed and the many like him who are in religious exile when I made my decision to let go of ordination. But I am now! At the time I was simply doing what I needed to do for my own integrity as a teacher. But Leed's words clarified something in me. They helped me realize more deeply that my own experience of exile was part of something much vaster than me. It is something that countless numbers of men and women in the world are experiencing today. That is why I am writing this book. I am writing for Leed and the many like him who are in exile. And I am writing also for many of my sisters and brothers who have chosen to remain in the church but who, like Leed, long for a spirituality of Earth's healing and humanity's wholeness. In my own life I straddle these two worlds, as do so many.

I feel part of the religious exile and at the same time I know how deeply rooted I am in my Christian inheritance. But whether we remain in the church or leave it, or follow a path somewhere in between, we are living in an age that is characterized by exile and spiritual search. Something new is trying to be born within us and among us.

Paul Tillich, the great twentieth-century German American theologian, prophetically anticipated this time of transition. In the last chapter of his collection of sermons, entitled *The Shaking of the Foundations*, he preached on words from the Prophecy of Isaiah, "I am about to do a new thing; now it springs forth; do you not perceive it?" (Isa. 43:19). What is the new thing that is trying to spring forth from within us and among us? He concluded by saying that if we think the new thing can only come through the old thing, then we are in danger of missing the new thing. He did not thereby mean that new spiritual vision and practice cannot come through the church. He did mean, however, that we are not to limit our hope of new beginnings to what may or may not happen in and through the existing traditions and practices of religion as we know them. The most we can do, he said, is to be ready and alert within ourselves for the new thing, whether it springs forth within the church or beyond it.

I don't see it as a coincidence that the turning point in my own journey of faith happened in the company of a rabbi. The Jewish people have known exile for most of their history. They have known its struggles and sufferings as well as its hopes and promises. Exile is a foundational theme running through the whole of Hebrew scripture, from beginning to end. Adam and Eve are exiled from the Garden of Eden, the place of their beginnings, to journey into territory they have never known. Abraham and Sarah choose self-exile from the land of their forebears in search of a country of promise. Moses and Miriam lead their people from captivity in Egypt into forty years in the desert before they find their land of freedom. And, finally, there is the Babylonian exile of the sixth century BCE following the siege of Jerusalem and the destruction of Solomon's Temple. "By the waters of Babylon, there we sat down, and there we wept when we remembered Zion" (Ps. 137:1). This Jewish song of yearning is perhaps the most archetypal expression of exile in scripture. It speaks of the universal longing for home. And home, of course, is not just a physical place. Most important, it is a spiritual place of deep identity in our souls and our relationship with Earth.

Martin Buber, the twentieth-century Jewish writer, and one of the great teachers that we will be drawing from in this book, said that there are epochs of being "at home" and epochs of "homelessness."[3] In particular, he was speaking about this in relation to his own people and their times of exile, but always when Buber speaks about the journey of his own people he is speaking also about the journey of humanity. Similarly, our story of religious exile today is part of a much bigger story. It is part of humanity's story of being in transition at this moment in time, seeking new vision, and searching for true relationship with Earth and one another.

The term that has been used historically to refer to the Jewish people in exile is diaspora. It comes from the Greek word *diasporá*, which is a compound of *dia*, meaning "through", and *sporá*, meaning "spores" or "seeds". Thus, diaspora refers to a people who have been scattered throughout the world. But they have not just been scattered. They are like seeds. They hold within themselves the promise of new life. So, when we speak of the African diaspora, for instance, the men and women of African descent who were scattered throughout the world by the slave trade, or the Celtic diaspora, the Scots and Irish who were forced from their homelands in the nineteenth century because of the Highland Clearances and the Potato Famine, or the Syrian diaspora and the Ukrainian diaspora of political refugees today, we are speaking not just about their scattering but about the seeds of new life that lie buried deep within them, waiting to spring forth in new ways and new interrelationships.

The Great Search: Turning to Earth and Soul in the Quest for Healing and Home is a book that recognizes the vast diaspora of men and women who have left traditional religion at this moment in time. But it is not just a matter of saying that many of us have been scattered from our religious homelands in an exile usually self-chosen in search of deeper meaning and truer relationship with Earth and one another. It is about the seeds of hope and promise that we carry within us.

This book of teachings from nine great figures of the past is about nurturing these seeds of hope and promise by turning to the Spirit within us and within the body of Earth for wisdom and guidance. Whether it is a Christian diaspora that we feel most immediately part of, or a Jewish or Muslim or Buddhist diaspora, at the end of the day, and at the deepest of levels, it is a human diaspora that we are part of. For it is humanity that is scattered and needs to be gathered back into true relationship with the spiritual depths of Earth and every human being again. This ultimately is what we are seeking, our true reconnection with Earth and one another, including a return to our own true depths individually.

"Seek and you will find," says Jesus. This is the promise that can lead us in our searching. It is a promise filled with hope for the urgent challenges of this moment in time as we open to the quest of the Spirit within us for healing and home.

PART ONE

One
Seeking Vision: Thomas Berry

Our vision needs to be as boundless as the cosmos, forever unfolding and inspired by the interrelatedness of all things. So taught the American Passionist priest Thomas Berry (1914–2009). Trained as a theologian, he preferred to call himself a "geologian", such was the place of Earth in his spiritual vision of reality. Berry offers an expansive vision to those of us seeking new beginnings today. It is a vision of hope in the face of the enormous challenges that confront religion, humanity, and Earth at this moment in time.

Berry's call to return to the divine includes a return to true relationship with Earth and every life-form, each species a unique expression of God. His vision was filled with ecological passion, denouncing humanity's abuses of Earth as well as announcing a way forward for the planet, for religion and the human species. He prophetically called this way forward the Ecozoic Age in which humanity would again learn to live in true and sustainable relationship with Earth.

Berry, who was born in North Carolina, spent most of his life in and around New York City, for some of that time teaching at Fordham University as well as directing the Riverdale Center of Religious Research along the Hudson River. He had a close relationship over the years with the Cathedral of St. John the Divine in the Morningside Heights neighbourhood of Manhattan, known especially for its St. Francis feast-day celebrations every autumn when the Cathedral includes in its liturgy a magnificent procession of creatures, ranging from camels and elephants to boa constrictors. It was there, during a winter solstice celebration of Paul Winter's Earth mass – the *Missa Gaia* – with its haunting wolf sounds, that Berry was inspired to write his poem "Morningside Cathedral":

We have heard in this Cathedral
Bach's Passion
The Lamentations of Jeremiah
Ancient experiences of darkness over the earth
Light born anew
But now, darkness deeper than even God
Can reach with a quick healing power
What sound,
What song,
What cry appropriate
What cry can bring a healing
When a million year rainfall
Can hardly wash away the life destroying stain?
What sound?
Listen – earth sound
Listen – the wind through the hemlock
Listen – the owl's soft hooting
in the winter night
Listen – the wolf – wolf song
Cry of distant meanings
woven into a seamless sound
Never before has the cry of the wolf expressed such meaning
On the winter mountainside
Morningside
This cry our revelation
As the sun sinks lower in the sky
Over our wounded world
The meaning of the moment
And the healing of the wound
Are there in a single cry
A throat open wide
For the wild sacred sound
Of some Great Spirit[1]

Berry was like a wolf crying out from the wilderness. His prophetic voice was "a throat open wide" calling us back into awareness of the universe as our home and challenging us as human beings to be guided by the interrelatedness of all things – religiously, economically, and politically. His cry was part of "the wild sacred sound of some Great Spirit" that is calling us back into true relationship with Earth and one another.

We sometimes speak of the "lone wolf", a phrase that refers to an individual who follows a path distinct from the well-trodden path of the majority. Berry's was again and again a lone voice calling prophetically from the edge of religion and society to give expression to a new vision of reality that saw the universe as essentially one and that viewed our healing in terms of coming back into sacred relationship with everything that has being. Out in the wilds of nature the lone wolf at times follows a solitary path for the sake of the pack, scouting the way forward for the well-being of the whole. Likewise, the lone path that Berry was prepared to tread in his life was a path that he followed for the sake of Earth and humanity, and for the renewal of the essential spirit of religion.

The cosmologist Brian Swimme, who worked closely with Berry in his unfolding vision, described him as "a person in the very midst of giving birth to a new order of human being ... a new planetary mode of being."[2] Holiness for him was about wholeness, living a life that reflected the holy interrelatedness of all things. Berry was a scholar of vast academic learning – culturally, historically, scientifically and spiritually – drawing from both East and West. And he combined this with a deep knowledge of myth, the world of dreams, and symbolic consciousness to imagine a new way forward for humanity. He believed that religion could play a creative role in helping lead us into well-being if we would again access religion's true spiritual depths. No other force has yet emerged in human history, he said, that "can so sustain us in adversity, so inspire us in moments of exaltation, or so awaken our imaginative and creative powers."[3]

Berry offers a threefold vision for the way in which religion can play a vital role in the healing of humanity, and thus come back into true relationship with the spiritual depths of its origins. First, he said, we are to move from a spirituality of alienation from the natural world to a spirituality of intimacy with the natural world. Second, we are to move from a spirituality of revelation through scripture to a spirituality of revelation through Earth. And third, we are to move from a spirituality of justice for human beings to a spirituality of justice for every life-form. "The destiny of Christianity," he said, "will be determined to a large extent by its capacity to fulfil these three commitments."[4]

The first path of Berry's threefold vision, then, is that we are to move from a spirituality of alienation from the natural world to a spirituality of intimacy with the natural world. He reminds us that we are "Earthlings", made of Earth.[5] This is our physical home as well as our spiritual home. And, at this moment in time, Earth is calling us back to itself in a new way, into a new intimacy, both physical and spiritual.

"We are most ourselves," said Berry, "when we are most intimate with the rivers and mountains and woodlands, with the sun and the moon and the stars in the heavens."[6] We are most ourselves when we are close to the ground that sustains us and the soil that grows our food. We have experienced the deep truth of this when we are closest to nature. The feeling of warm sunshine on our skin, the sight of the full moon rising in the night sky, the breathing in of fresh mountain air, the experience of wild seas around us, the taste of a potato newly dug from the ground. These experiences of intimacy with nature make us feel more well and more connected to the ground from which we and all things have come. We need a new "rapport" with the planet, says Berry.[7] We need to rediscover what he calls "the mystique of Earth" and open our eyes again to the child's way of seeing, remembering what we knew in our infancy, a light-filled universe, a physical world flooded with the radiance of spirit.[8]

And because this is our home, then what we do to the natural world is what we do to ourselves, including our souls. It is not just our lungs and bodies that are damaged by particle and light pollution in the cities. It is "soul-deprivation", says Berry.[9] To not be able to see the stars is a deprivation of our inner world, a loss of wonder, and thus a diminishing of our imagination and the ability to remember our origins in the heavens and to dream our way forward into new beginnings on Earth.

Thus, Berry calls for an "exodus" from our captivity to worldviews that have pretended humanity could be well by ignoring or dominating the natural world rather than by learning from the natural world and living in intimacy with it.[10] Our existing traditions, whether religious or political or cultural, have been unequal to the task. They have been unable to prevent the ecological crises that threaten the very future of humanity. We therefore need a new liberation, a second flight from Egypt, as it were, a release from our captivity to religious and political systems that alienate us from Earth, setting humanity over and against the natural world rather than into deeper relationship with it. It is freedom from captivity to the prevailing empires of thought and belief and consumerism in the Western world that will enable us to discover new ways of relating to Earth as the very ground of our well-being.

We are living in the midst of a growing Earth consciousness and connection with the interrelationship of all things. Hand in hand with this consciousness is a growing "woman consciousness", says Berry.[11] Earth consciousness and woman consciousness are inseparably related. "The fate of the one," he said, "is the fate of the other."[12] The way Earth has been subordinated and abused over the centuries is the way women have been subordinated and abused in so much of our cultural and religious history. A recovery of reverence for the one will be accompanied by a recovery of reverence for the other. They belong inseparably together.

We need a balance among all genders in the world, including within our religious traditions and leadership. And if this balance is to be achieved, said Berry, perhaps we need a period of accentuated feminine emphasis to redress the imbalance that has crippled humanity for centuries. The human journey desperately needs to be under the inspiration and care and direction of women as well as men. This alone will free us from the shadow masculine energies that have dominated our power structures of religion and society, resulting in the tragic alienation from Earth that imperils our future.

Berry's call for a spirituality of intimacy with Earth is a call that had been anticipated in nineteenth century America by teachers like Ralph Waldo Emerson and Henry David Thoreau, and by the Celtic prophet John Muir. They too saw a physical world that was imbued with spirit. Berry's call for intimacy with Earth, however, moves even deeper by including the findings of new science and its understanding of the essential interrelatedness of everything in the universe. And his vision is deepened also by the way he draws on the ancient wisdom of humanity's spiritual traditions, bringing together East and West.

Berry believed there are ways of seeing deep in our religious inheritance that are still to be fully realized and articulated. This is a moment, he said, when the deepest meanings of our ancient traditions of belief should emerge to enable a new vision of faith in the universe. Religion has changed considerably over the centuries. There have been moments of great transition in the past. We are living in a time that is calling for even greater change. Our religion – with its rituals, symbols and myths – is not as fixed and unyielding as it might appear. It is as adaptable as life, said Berry, for its very origins are deep in the body of Earth. Religion, like life itself, is given to evolve and find ever-new expression.

Christianity for most of its history has been excessively oriented toward transcendence, to the above-ness or beyond-ness of the divine. It needs now to recover its orientation toward immanence and the within-ness of the divine. At the heart of the Christian tradition is the story of incarnation, of God born in the flesh. But what have we done with this radical story of the divine-human intermingling in the Christ

Child? We have said it points only to one, Jesus, rather than to all. We have treated him as an exception to humanity and as an exception to the universe, rather than as a revelation of humanity and Earth, all flesh, all matter interpenetrated with spirit. The cherished song of Immanuel that has echoed down through the centuries within the walls of Christianity needs now to be sung clearly and emphatically as a song of the immanence of the divine in all things, pointing not simply to the divine with us in one person, one place and one time but to the divine within us in every person, every place and every time.

Christianity for most of its history has also tended to focus exclusively on divine-human relations and interhuman relations, calling us into relationship with God in a way that also includes true relationship with one another. Love God and love your neighbour as yourself. What needs to come forth now is a focus also on human-Earth relations and on every species as our neighbour. Love God and love every species as yourself. This is the deep challenge of this moment in time.

Berry believed that a new interaction between the divine, the human and Earth has begun. We are in a time of transition moving from a theology of religion and an anthropology of religion toward the beginnings also of a cosmology of religion, a celebration of Earth and the universe as a single sacred community within which we will find our true well-being. Christian teaching over the centuries has beautifully expressed a vision of faithfulness to God and faithfulness to humanity. The new articulation that must now come forth clearly is faithfulness to Earth. This will be the critical defining feature of a reborn Christianity for today.

And it is not just from within our own religious tradition that we are to look for wisdom to face the great challenges of this moment. It is from every great religious tradition of humanity. Each tradition has a unique and distinctive offering to make toward the well-being of humanity. We need one another as religious traditions as much as the species of Earth need one another to be well. Religious diversity, in which each tradition is allowed to remain inviolably itself, is as important to the human soul as biodiversity is to the planet.

Berry, as a professor in the History of Religions graduate programme at Fordham University from 1966 to 1979, delved deeply into Eastern thought to complement the wisdom of his own religious inheritance. In response to the 1965 Vatican II document *Nostra Aetate* ("In Our Time"), which was considered a radical statement in its affirmation of the "rays of truth" that can be glimpsed in other religious traditions, Berry said it is not just rays of truth that we find in other religions, it is "floods of illumination".[13] It is the brilliant spiritual insights of other traditions as well as the deep wisdom of our own that we need to look to if our vision is to be true to the essential oneness and interrelatedness of the universe.

And of paramount importance at this moment in time is to look especially to the indigenous traditions of the world, including the native wisdoms of our own inheritance, like the Celtic stream of wisdom within Christian thought. These are the traditions, says Berry, that can most deeply help us recover a vision of humanity's relationship with Earth as sacred. In indigenous spiritual wisdom the natural world is viewed as "Thou", says Berry, not as "It".[14] Everything in nature is to be related to with reverence, not simply used or exploited. In native wisdom the world is "a communion of subjects", he says, not "a collection of objects".[15] Well-being will be found through the way of communion with Earth rather than through the way of conquest of Earth.

As European nations historically conquered native peoples and native lands throughout the world, again and again religious leaders insisted on conformity to our ways, little knowing that it was we as colonizers who needed to be taught their ways in relation to living reverently and sustainably with Earth. Dialogue with native peoples is urgently needed today. They are the ones who hold a model of sacred relationship with Earth and can help guide us in our search for new beginnings.

Years ago, during a visit to the Cree Nation in northern Saskatchewan in Canada, a native leader shared with me "The Grandmother's

Creation Story", which in Cree mythology recounts the journey of humanity in relation to Earth.[16] After the rivers, forests and mountains were formed, and every plant and animal had emerged from the ground, humanity was born. But because human beings were weaker than many of the creatures of Earth, the Creator instructed the animals to watch over humanity and guide them in their ways. The day came, however, when one of the human beings, a man, took more food than he required. Discord now came between the animal world and the human world, and men waged war on the creatures. It was at this time that human beings began to forget the language of the creatures and thus the ability to learn from them. But in compassion the Creator made spirit-animals that would visit men and women in their dreams at night and in their imaginations by day to whisper wisdom to those whose ears were still open. Thus began the healing of the wound.

"Listen," writes Berry, "wolf song, cry of distant meanings ... and the healing of the wound." It is Earth sound that Berry invites us to listen to again, to open to the wisdom of the creatures, the trees, the rivers, the mountains. Earth sound comes to us like the wind through hemlock, like the owl's soft hooting in the night, like the wolf's wild cry under the whiteness of the moon. It is a cry of revelation to our wounded world, says Berry, beckoning us back into intimacy with Earth. It is "the wild sacred sound of some Great Spirit".

The second imperative in Berry's threefold vision of how religion can play a vital role in the future journey of humanity is that we are to move from a spirituality of revelation through scripture to a spirituality of revelation through Earth. Berry is inviting us to return to the natural world as the place of our primary revelatory experience of the divine. Humanity was consulting the sacred text of Earth and the heavens long before written scriptures came into being. And some of the earliest expressions of written scripture were simply transcriptions of what was being read in Earth and the skies.

Berry's call to return to nature as our original place of revelation is not to entirely dismiss the place of the Bible in our Judeo-Chistian inheritance, although Berry did wonder if we need to place scripture on the shelf for a while until we can come back into true relationship with the cosmos as our first and primary source of revelation. There have been times in the history of Western Christianity, during the sixteenth-century Reformation in Europe, for instance, when Christian teachers taught *Sola Scriptura*, scripture alone, as the source of revelation. And much of the Protestant world today has been heavily influenced by this way of thinking. Berry is challenging us to recover the forgotten and tragically neglected place of the natural world in our revelatory experience of the divine.

It was primarily after his retirement from Fordham University in 1979, as he more and more focused his attention on the work of the Riverdale Center of Religious Research, that Berry's voice became emphatic about the need to return to Earth and the cosmos as our principal source of revelation. And it is interesting to note that his most creative prophetic articulations did not occur until he was more than seventy years old! His seminal work, *The Dream of the Earth*, was published in 1988, after which came *The Great Work* in 1999, *The Christian Future and the Fate of Earth* in 2009, and his final major publication, *The Sacred Universe*, also published in 2009. Berry was now gathering around himself postdoctoral theological students like Mary Evelyn Tucker and John Grim (who later headed up the Forum on Religion and Ecology at Yale University) and young scientists like Brian Swimme, who subsequently coauthored *Journey of the Universe*. This was the next generation of women and men to take forward Berry's vision of Earth's sacredness. They spoke of him as a gentle and mesmerizing presence whose countenance shone with passion and kindness when he spoke. Swimme said that listening to him was like having an "altered state" of consciousness experience. "We all fell in love," said Swimme. "With sunshine – with the rising of the moon ... With everything. And certainly with each other ... You would find yourself simply overwhelmed with a desire to get married. With anyone nearby. Did I say with anyone? I meant with everyone. With the Great Red Oak sheltering the library. Even with the sky overhead."[17]

But, of course, there were others who regarded him as a dangerous thinker in his radical challenges of tradition and his call for change. Berry managed to stay under the radar of the Vatican's Congregation for the Doctrine of the Faith (formerly called the Inquisition) by quietly offering his teachings from the Riverdale Center and by avoiding major publication of his work until relatively late in life. There were young priests and religious sisters, however, who were only able to come and see him by claiming that they were coming to him for personal confession. And as one sister put it to me, "Quite often it was group confession." It was in these small gatherings at Riverdale that a new vision of reality was being forged. In time this vision came to be called the Universe Story. It was a way of speaking of the origins of life as both physical and spiritual, and of the beginnings and purpose of all things as sacred.

The key for Berry was story. "It's all a question of story," he said. "We are in trouble just now because we do not have a good story. We are in between stories. The Old Story – the account of how the world came to be and how we fit into it – is not functioning properly, and we have not learned the New Story."[18] Not yet anyway. This is what Berry and his young cohorts were working on.

For Berry there were three main texts to draw from in developing the New Story – the cosmic text of the universe, the written text of scripture, and the interior text of the human soul. All three, he believed, were essential to the makings of "a good story". He saw clearly that we are at a critical juncture in the history of humanity and the evolution of religion. The New Story needs to be deeply true to this moment in time and to speak powerfully into it.

First then, he said, there is the cosmic text, the body of Earth, and every galaxy in the universe. The whole cosmos is like a living scripture that we need to read and listen to if we are to learn how to tell the sacred story of our origins and purpose for today. The universe has been a spiritual as well as a physical reality from the very beginning, said Berry. Not to hear the natural world is not to hear the divine. Much of our Western culture and religion has been "autistic", he said, in relation to the nonhuman world.[19] Especially after the seventeenth century with the rise of philosophical rationalism, we spiritually withdrew from relationship with animal life and plant life, assuming that consciousness was a feature only of humanity rather than of every life-form. We stripped the natural world of its spiritual qualities. And it became to us an unenchanted universe, devoid of soul. Berry calls us back into reverent relationship with Earth, allowing the entire body of the universe to become once more a living sacred text.

Second, there is the text of written scriptures in the religious traditions of humanity. These sometimes point to the sacredness of the cosmos, but their primary focus is on divine-human relationship and interhuman relationship. Certainly, this is the case with scripture in the Judeo-Christian tradition with its prophetic emphasis on right relationship with God and with one another, including a passionate concern for justice and a defence of those who are powerless. But the biblical story as it now stands, said Berry, however unique and important in its expression, is not sufficient to address the most critical issues of this moment in time. It has become a "sectarian story" in its failure to profoundly tell the story of Earth and to provide a clear vision for the way forward for humanity.[20]

And third, there is the interior text of the human soul, that place of inner wisdom in us that we can consult in our search for what is true and beautiful, as well as just and loving. It is in the interior text of the human soul that we can access gifts of the imagination and vision for the path ahead. If we are to tell a New Story, rather than simply trying to patch up the Old Story, then we need both the cosmic text of our origins as well as the interior text of the human soul to be able to dream the way forward. All three texts are essential to the creation of a New Story. They will enable us to tell not only the divine-human story and the interhuman story but the human-Earth story, and to do so with hope and vision.

Berry and his young colleagues began increasingly to speak of this New Story as the Universe Story. It was a way of remembering that our personal story, like the story of everything that has being in the universe, began 13.7 billion years ago with a great flaring forth of light. That is when I began and that is when you began. Within less than a second the universe started its rapid expansion, which now extends 46 billion light years in every direction. Not that we are the centre. It is an omni-centric universe. Are we looking *up* into the night skies when we gaze at the moon and the shining constellations? Or are we looking *down* into the night skies? The centre is everywhere. Humanity was born in a galaxy that would eventually be called the Milky Way. We now know, however, that there are billions of galaxies, each with billions of stars. And every single particle in this ever-unfolding universe is related to every other particle.

Berry wanted us to be amazed, constantly amazed, by this one, single, interrelated body of the universe that new science describes as a single multiform reality, or as "Undivided Wholeness in Flowing Movement".[21] It just keeps flowing and flowing into ever-new form. Four and a half billion years ago it flowed into the form of a planet of burning molten rock. And over the course of four billion years this globe of burning rock, Earth as it was later called, has transformed itself into birds and bees and butterflies, and into the emergence of human thought and music and love. We are each a shining flow of sacred energy.

Homo sapiens, meaning wise one, appeared 200,000 years ago. We are latecomers in this story. The term "wise ones" does not accurately describe what we have been to one another and to Earth, but it could yet describe what we will become. As Berry adds, there is good reason to hope that "the Universe is for us rather than against us".[22] Given the dangerous moments that have been navigated thus far in the unfolding story of humanity and Earth, there is good reason to hope. It is now up to us to live from the wisdom of the Spirit that is deep within us.

*

The final part of Berry's threefold vision of how religion can play its part in the healing of Earth and humanity is that we are to move from a spirituality of justice for human beings to a spirituality of justice for every life-form. Humanity and Earth will go into the future together, he believed, or we will not go into the future at all. There are not two worlds, the world of the human and the world of the nonhuman. "There is a single world," he said. "We will live or die as this world lives or dies."[23]

This was Berry prepared to use "apocalyptic language", as he called it. Apocalyptic language needs to be employed in communicating to humanity because it is we who are responsible for the widespread degradation of Earth that is occurring. Berry's life spanned almost a century. Over this time, he witnessed the acceleration of the primary factors contributing to the ecological crises that threaten the future of humanity – population growth, the extinction of species, deforestation, climate change, and the severe loss of biodiversity. When Berry was born, the world population was less than two billion. It now stands at nearly eight billion. Similarly, the extinction of species has increased rapidly over the past century, to the point that we are now experiencing what scientists call an "extinction spasm" on Earth.[24] The UN Convention on Biological Diversity estimates that every day up to one hundred and fifty species are being ripped for ever out of the fabric of life. This is more than one thousand times higher than Earth's natural rate of extinction. And since Berry's birth in 1914, the world has lost as much natural forest as would cover the entire landmass of the United States. Much of this has been driven by the development of meat production on a vast industrial scale, clearing upwards of eighty thousand acres of tropical rainforest every day to maintain humanity's excessive levels of meat consumption. Berry was alert to the magnitude of these problems early on, and he challenged humanity and religion to respond.

Our "pathology", as he called it, consists of a tragic discontinuity between the human world and the nonhuman world, in which humanity has been given all the inherent value and all the controlling rights, whereas Earth's other life-forms have been given none or little.[25] This has been true in nearly every major sphere of human life, whether political and economic, or intellectual and religious. And this discontinuity was born primarily out of a biblical-Christian matrix in the Western world, rather than out of Eastern worldviews like Buddhism and Hinduism. There was something "susceptible" in our Christian tradition to being used this way, said Berry, because of its anthropocentric exaltation of humanity over Earth's other life-forms.[26] It allowed, for instance, someone like the prominent seventeenth-century philosopher Francis Bacon to say quite uninhibitedly that we are to put nature "on the rack" to force her to yield up her secrets for the advantage of humanity.[27] And this is exactly what the Western world has chosen to do over the centuries, and the consequences are dire.

Berry used apocalyptic language to awaken humanity to the danger. As his teacher, the French Celtic theologian and scientist Pierre Teilhard de Chardin, taught, either we "see" or we "perish".[28] Apocalyptic language wakes us up to see by raising the alarm, but Berry also knew that we need more than the language of fear. We also need the language of hope. And, so, Berry offered us a vision of hope. He promised the coming of a new age, if we would transition from a place of dominating Earth's life-forms to a place of living mutually in beneficial relationship with them, allowing the other species of Earth not only to survive but to flourish. This would enable us to rediscover what he called "the ancient law of reciprocity" in which the part will truly thrive only if the whole is allowed to thrive.[29] Humanity will be well if Earth's other life-forms are allowed to be well. The natural world will bring about its own healing, he said, if we allow it to do so, if "we permit it to function within the dynamics of its own genius".[30] This is the "Great Work", he said, that lies ahead of humanity today.

✻

We are living in "a moment of grace", said Berry.[31] Moments of grace are privileged moments, for great transformations can occur if we are true to them. Humanity's discovery of how to make fire was a moment of grace, as was the invention of spoken language or the first cultivation of a garden or the development of writing and the creation of an alphabet. Humanity seized these moments of grace and brought great change through them.

We too are living in a moment of grace. It is the realization of the interrelatedness of all things. It is a consciousness rising to the fore in nearly every great discipline of thought and study, inviting us to know that what we do to a part we do to the whole, and that the well-being of each is fulfilled only in the well-being of the whole. But moments of grace, said Berry, are "transient".[32] In other words, if we miss them, they are gone, perhaps never to come again. Will we meet this moment and live into it deeply, applying the new consciousness of Earth's oneness to our lives and relationships, or will we miss this moment?

The universe is so amazing, said Berry, that it must have been dreamt into being. And we are in such turmoil – ecologically, politically, religiously – we are in such a mess that we need to dream the way forward. We need to allow ourselves to imagine new ways of being, new ways of seeing, new ways of relating to one another and Earth. This, he said, is the "Great Work" that we are being invited to be part of today, to bring our deepest energies and the deepest spiritual insights of our inheritance to this moment in time, that we may be part of truly meeting this moment of grace together.[33]

Earth sound comes down to us from the beginning of time. It is calling to us today with a new urgency in the rivers and mountains, in the trees and creatures. If only we could hear, as Berry said in his poem "Morningside Cathedral". If only we could open to the wolf

> … as guardian spirit. As saviour guide?
> Our Jeremiah, telling us,
> Not about the destruction of
> Jerusalem or its temple
> Our Augustine, telling us,
> not about the destruction of Rome and civilization
> Our Bach,
> telling us not about the Passion of Christ in ancient times,
> But about the Passion of Earth in our times?
> Wolf – our earth, our Christ, ourselves.
> The arch of the Cathedral itself takes on the shape
> Of the uplifted throat of the wolf
> Lamenting our present destiny
> Beseeching humankind
> To bring back the sun
> To let the flowers bloom in the meadows,
> The rivers run through the hills
> And let the Earth
> And all its living creatures
> Live their
> Wild,
> Fierce,
> Serene
> And Abundant life.[34]

MEDITATIVE PRACTICE: SEEKING VISION

Thomas Berry is a messenger of vision to us. He invites us to see everything in the universe as both physical and spiritual, and to see that we all began 13.7 billion years ago in the great flaring forth of light. This is our shared story. Will we learn to live it together with the other species of Earth? Or will we continue to pretend that there are two stories, one for humanity and one for the rest of the planet, thus endangering both? It is together that we will flourish.

(pause to listen for what Berry's wisdom stirs in us)

As the darkness of early morning longs for light
so my soul longs to see again
the great spiritual fire of life's beginnings
still shining
in galaxies beyond numbering
and here in me and every lifeform
countless streams of glory in a single flow of light
each one irreplaceable.

(pause to be aware)

As the darkness of early morning longs for light
so my soul longs to see again.

Two

Seeking Earth: Nan Shepherd

We are living in the midst of a growing consciousness of Earth. As we have already noted, nearly every great discipline of thought is pointing us to the interrelatedness of all things and to humanity's need to live sustainably with Earth and all its life-forms. From the study of ecology and economy to that of psychology and spirituality, the message is clear, Earth's well-being and our well-being are inseparably related. The Scottish writer Nan Shepherd (1893–1981) intuitively anticipated this consciousness. As early as the first half of the twentieth century, her writings articulated a vision of Earth's sacredness. Seeking true relationship with Earth, both physically and spiritually, is central to the Great Search of this moment in time. Shepherd announced the heart of this search early on, and her words continue to nurture it today.

She is known especially for her love of the Scottish mountains, particularly the Cairngorm Mountains range at the heart of the Highlands in Scotland. She saw that everything can be viewed as a revelation of light. It is a light that shines deep in the matter of Earth and every life-form. Of the mountains themselves, she writes, light is their "making" as well as their "substance".[1] Not only are they made by light, they are composed of light. As is humanity. We too shine with this same spiritual substance that is on fire, she says. And, alluding to the story of the burning bush in Hebrew scripture in which Moses encounters a desert shrub that is on fire with the light of the divine without being consumed, Shepherd speaks of the light that shines in the human countenance and the light that burns in the landscape of the natural world as "the bush burning and not consumed".[2] Deep within all things is the sacred fire of our essence.

Shepherd first appeared on the Scottish literary scene in the late 1920s. Between 1928 and 1934 she produced three novels and a book of poetry that played a significant part in Scotland's literary revival of the early twentieth century. Then, after this six-year burst of creativity, there came nothing for the longest time. As she confessed to her close friend, the author Neil Gunn, "I've gone dumb … I suppose there's nothing for it but to go on living. Speech may come. Or it may not. And if it doesn't, I suppose one has just to be content to be dumb. At least not shout for the mere sake of making a noise."[3] But eventually speech did come again. And this time it came in what was to be her greatest piece of writing, *The Living Mountain*. To begin with, however, no one wanted it. In 1945 she completed a draft of the book, in which she describes her relationship with the Cairngorm Mountains as a love affair. These were the peaks and glens at the heart of the Scottish Highlands that she walked year after year from her house in Deeside, in every season, snow or sunshine, by day and at night, usually alone but sometimes with friends and companions. She found that the mountains were perpetually new to her every time she returned to them. They hold "astonishment for me," she said. "There is no getting accustomed to them."[4] And it was an appetite that grew with the feeding, she says, "like drink and passion". So much so that she was considered "fey", or a little mad, by those who could not understand why she was entering the mountains in every weather and season.[5]

At the heart of Shepherd's knowing of the Cairngorms was her realization that the whole of the mountain range is "one and indivisible", as she put it, including all its life-forms and constituent elements. "All are aspects of one entity," she said. "The disintegrating rock, the nurturing rain, the quickening sun, the root, the bird – all are one." Together they form what she calls "the living mountain".[6] This was to become Shepherd's metaphor for the oneness and interrelatedness of Earth. We and all life-forms, including the elements of earth, air, fire, and water, are one and indivisible. Together we form Earth.

In 1945 Shepherd approached a Scottish publisher with a view to getting her book published. She received a courteous but negative reply, so she placed the manuscript into a drawer and didn't take it out again for more than thirty years. As an old woman, while tidying up her possessions, she rediscovered the rejected manuscript and, on reading it once more, realized that her tale of love for the mountain was as vital then as it had been upon first writing. She thus sent it off to Aberdeen University Press for consideration. In 1977 it was quietly published as *The Living Mountain*. Today it is an international bestseller. Her words are giving voice to the human quest for true relationship with Earth. And she is being celebrated in her homeland by ecologists, feminists, poets and artists alike. A photograph of the young Nan Shepherd now appears on the Scottish five-pound note. The author who feared she had gone dumb is being honoured in Scotland as the first-ever female writer to be so recognized. She represents the recovery of reverence for Earth and reverence for womanhood that is so vital to our well-being.

Shepherd's knowing of the mountain became more and more feminine in its expression over the years. She came to see that it was not a matter of conquering the peaks or taking the summits, as so much mountain literature written by men makes us aspire to. For her it was more like a pilgrimage into the mountain, longing simply to be in its presence. In the early years, she admits, she had sought "the sensation of height" or "the sensation of effort". But this, she said, was just lust and pride. At that point "I was not interested in the mountain for itself, but for its effect upon me," she said. In time, however, she came simply to love the mountain, its glens as well as its heights, its recesses as well as its peaks, a journey that took many years to mature and never stopped unfolding. "Knowing another is endless," as she put it. "The thing to be known grows with the knowing."[7] And the relationship can never be rushed. "Haste can do nothing with these hills," she says.[8] Their formation has taken millions of years. We are simply to be present to the mountain and learn to encounter it the way a lover comes to know the beloved. Often it will give itself to us most completely when we have no fixed destination in mind but have simply gone out to be with it in love. Shepherd calls this way of knowing, living in "the present tense" or practising "the grammar of now".[9] For it is now, always now, that the essence of Earth is waiting to reveal itself to us.

Some of this knowing came to Shepherd through the intimacy of sleep, literally sleeping in the hills and valleys like a lover falling to sleep in the arms of the beloved. No one knows the mountain completely, she said, who has not slept with it. "As one slips into sleep, the mind grows limpid; the body melts; perception alone remains. One neither thinks, nor desires, nor remembers, but dwells in pure intimacy with the tangible world." It was in these moments of "quiescent perceptiveness", as she called them, that she most deeply came to know the mountain, knowing not simply with her mind but with her whole being.[10]

Shepherd loved daytime sleep in the hills as much as sleeping in the wild at night. In the warmth of the midday sun, after an early start to the day of hiking, she would lie on the mountain plateau and slip in and out of sleep, "one of the sweetest luxuries in life," she said. Falling to sleep on the mountain has the corollary of course of waking on the mountain. And because outdoor sleep is often deeper than normal sleep, there is sometimes that startled moment, writes Shepherd, when you wake and look at a familiar place as though you had never seen it before. It is like a recapturing of early childhood's "pristine amazement" at first witnessing the wonder of light.[11]

To sleep outside, even for a few minutes, can have the effect of "uncoupling the mind", says Shepherd. She found that as she half woke in the hills, she was free from thought, as she described it, free even from thinking about the mountain because she was simply being present to it and one with it. "At no other moment," she writes, "am I sunk quite so deep into its life. I have let go my self." In those moments she is not bound by self-consciousness, for she is aware not primarily of her distinctness from the mountain but of her oneness with the mountain. And she finds herself "as tranquil as the stones, rooted far down in their immobility." To thus move in and out of sleep on the mountain, coming to the surface of awareness again and again is to live "in the clear simplicity of the senses," she says.[12]

The clear simplicity of the senses. On the mountain Shepherd experiences a perception so pure that "the body may be said to think," she says.[13] This is the way of knowing that she invites us back into. And it is a way of relationship not only with the mountain but with Earth and its countless life-forms, including one another. It is to know with all our senses as well as with our head, body-knowing not just mind-knowing. To her friend Neil Gunn, she writes, it is the whole of our body that we must use "to instruct the spirit".[14] Each of the senses is a way into what Earth wants to teach us and show us and give us.

The studio portrait of Shepherd as a young woman that is used on the Royal Bank of Scotland five-pound note makes her look slightly Native American in appearance. Her hair, parted down the middle, is braided on either side. And across her forehead is a broad headband with a jewel set in the centre. The reality, however, as she explained years later, is that she was just fooling around at the photographer's and picked up a piece of film in the studio and placed it round her head with a brooch stuck on the front. But the portrait anticipates a way of knowing that she was later to give expression to in her writing and embody in her life. It is a way of knowing that invites a deep respect again for the native wisdom that every culture has known early in its history, an intuitive and instinctive knowing of Earth that comes through the senses. Shepherd invites us to expand our knowing, to again use the body to instruct the spirit. "This is the innocence we have lost," she said.[15] Our body no longer thinks.

The Living Mountain is a summons to reawaken to the senses. "I am like a dog," writes Shepherd, "smells excite me."[16] Similarly, Shepherd speaks of the fragrance of birch after rainfall. "It is a scent with body to it," she writes, "fruity like old brandy, and on a wet warm day, one can be as good as drunk with it."[17] Also, the sound of silence in the hills. Listening to it, one slips out of time. "Such silence is not a mere negation of sound," she says. "It is like a new element."[18]

But it is not always silence and stillness that one hears in the mountain. The ears can listen also to wildness and storm. "Gales crash," she says, "with the boom of angry seas: one can hear the air shattering itself upon rock. Cloud-bursts batter the earth and roar down the ravines, and thunder reverberates with a prolonged and menacing roll."[19] The sound of such elemental tumult carries an energy that has been at work in the universe for millions of years. It is awe-inspiring. But never is Shepherd naive to the danger of elemental forces in the mountain. Every year lives are lost in its wild storms and low-hanging mists. When dark rain invades body and soul, she writes, the mountain can become a frightening place. Awe is an essential part of truly knowing Earth.

But of all the senses, it is eye and touch that hold the greatest potency for Shepherd. "How can I number the worlds to which the eye gives me entry," she writes, "the world of light, of colour, of shape, of shadow: of mathematical precision in the snowflake, the ice formation, the quartz crystal, the patterns of stamen and petal … and [the] plunging line of the mountain face."[20] For Shepherd it is like a love feast, gazing at every feature and contour of the body of the beloved. Its waters enthrall her with their flash and gleam, their pliancy and grace. "Water, that strong white stuff," she writes, "one of the four elemental mysteries, can here be seen at its origins. Like all profound mysteries, it is so simple that it frightens me. It wells from the rocks [at the top of the mountain] and flows away. For unnumbered years it has welled from the rocks and flowed away. It does nothing, absolutely nothing, but be itself."[21] Being. The mountain invites her to be. And to let go to the flow of light that courses deep in the body of her being and the body of Earth. This is what pilgrimage into the heart of the natural world does to us. It invites us to be.

The flaming colours of autumn, she says, are each year more astonishing than she expects. Or the glowing purple of birch trees in the spring when the sap rises, "how trunks and boughs and smallest twigs light up."[22] And not only in the spring but throughout the year. "From its February purple to its golden fall ... the birch is a study in colour that provides endless delight."[23] Shepherd looks for colour even in the grey granite of Scotland's hills and mountains, especially at sunrise or sunset when they can glow deep red with reflection. "When I hear strangers call our country grey," she writes, "I do not necessarily contradict; for if grey is the universal solvent, melting all colours into itself, *looking* will resolve them back [again]. Our grey land, our grey skies, hold poised within them a thousand shades of colour."[24] If we look with wonder and love, she says, we will find endless delight even in the greyness of Earth's body.

But it is touch, the touch of the beloved, that is the most intimate sense of all. She speaks of the "benediction" of walking barefoot in the mountains, feeling the moistness of Earth beneath her feet. And the "infinity of pleasure" that comes to her through touch, tracing the soft curves and hard outlines of Earth's body with her hands.[25] This is where her language becomes most sensuous, "naked birch trees", "naked hands", "naked legs", the "slap [of water] against my body".[26] Her relationship with the mountain is intimate. "The whole sensitive skin is played upon," she writes, "the whole body ... answers to the thrust of forces incomparably stronger than itself." And after rain, she continues, "I run my hand through juniper or birches for the joy of the wet drops trickling over the palm or walk through long heather to feel its wetness on my naked legs."[27]

Shepherd does not explicitly mention an intimacy of human relationship in her life. And she never married. But in her poem "An Ecstasy Remembered", she points to the memory of what may have been a secret encounter, "the shining moment of our ecstasy", as she calls it, a hidden time in a wood that she describes as a place where "the bare wet birches stood". She calls it "our moment of amazed beatitude".[28] But whether there was such a person and such a place of encounter or not, there is no doubt that Shepherd knew the passion of love in her life. Her love affair with the mountain was deep and sensuous and abiding. And it is a love affair that she invites us to know in our own lives, to open to our own shining moments of ecstasy with the natural world, that we too may deepen our passion for Earth.

Shepherd describes her relationship with the mountain as a "traffic of love".[29] By this she means that in the presence of the mountain she is forever travelling back and forth between the outer landscape of the natural world and the inner landscape of the soul. The physical in all its grandeur, wildness, stillness, wetness, sunshine, transported her through her senses into the unseen and eternal world of spirit within her. And this journey between the outer and the inner, the physical and the spiritual, was a journey of love. For it is love that most immediately opens the door between the physical and the spiritual just as in the intimacy of human relationship it is love that can make the physical knowing of the other an "amazed beatitude", a sacrament of the eternal.

Shepherd describes hiking for the first time to Loch Avon, a remote mountain loch set deep in the Cairngorm plateau. She and her walking companion arrived around midday when the sun penetrated most directly into the waters. "We stripped and bathed," she writes. "The clear water was at our knees, then at our thighs … What we saw under water had a sharper clarity than what we saw through air. We waded on into the brightness … Then I looked down: and at my feet there opened a gulf of brightness so profound that the mind stopped." Shepherd unexpectedly finds herself standing at the edge of an underwater precipice that suddenly drops one hundred feet to the bottom of the loch. In that moment, she writes, "my spirit was as naked as my body. It was one of the most defenceless moments of my life."[30]

In part it is the fear of physical danger that seizes her in the waters of the loch. She wasn't a swimmer so any imbalance on the underwater ledge might have been perilous to her. But the experience also transports her into the inner realm. "My spirit was as naked as my body." Below her in the mountain loch is a brightness of depth she had not imagined. It is beautiful and it is also terrifying. In that moment, she senses the unfathomable depths of the waters of her soul. To be in touch with the wildness of the natural world, in its heights and depths, can also be to open our senses to the unplumbed depths of our inner being and its mystery of light forever shimmering from deep within us. This was the sort of journeying that characterized Shepherd's life. It was a pilgrimage into the soul. She did some world travel over the years, to places like South Africa and Greece, but it was her inner journey of love with the mountain that most distinguishes her spirit and her writings. She in fact only ever lived in the small village of West Cults in Aberdeenshire. And, in an interview late in life, she boasted playfully about having had the same bedroom all her life. Even her work only ever took her to nearby Aberdeen, to the Training Centre for Teachers, where for forty-one years she taught English literature to young women aspiring to be schoolteachers. Shepherd's own description of her role at the college, however, was "the heaven-appointed task" of trying to prevent at least a few of these young women from conforming altogether to the approved patterns of society.[31] Never a conformist. Always rather more like a bird flying free into the wilds of the mountain and the untamed spirit of the feminine.

Shepherd often hiked alone in the vast expanses of the Cairngorms, but sometimes she walked with others, including students from Aberdeen. Alone or with others, however, it was always silence that she most preferred in hiking. The presence of another person does not necessarily detract from the experience of silence. It can even enhance the silence if the other is "the right sort of hill companion", as she put it.[32] But the most important thing is to allow our identity to merge with the mountain. That way any conversation that arises is "lit up from within by contact with it," she said.[33] Not that the conversation needs to be about the mountain. It needs simply to be one with the mountain. Always what Shepherd set out to achieve in entering the mountain, whether on her own or in the company of others, was what she called an "accession of interiority", moving in awareness from the outer landscape around her to an awareness also of the inner landscape of her soul.[34] This is what our experience of communion with Earth can do for us. It opens the door between the inner and the outer, and between the human soul and the soul of Earth.

Shepherd had what has been described as a talent for "untroubling silences".[35] Whether walking with friends in the Cairngorms or meeting them on the High Street of Old Aberdeen, she was comfortable with silence. And it was often accompanied by a twinkle in the eye. This had the effect of setting others at ease in silence with her. For it wasn't that she was embarrassed or inhibited or didn't have anything to say. It was simply that "to listen is better than to speak," as she put it.[36]

But speak she did, thank God, especially in her writings. "So there I lie on the plateau," she writes in describing one of her journeys into the Cairngorms, "under me the central core of fire from which was thrust this grumbling grinding mass of plutonic rock, over me blue air and between the fire of the rock and the fire of the sun, soil and water, moss, grass, flower and tree, insect, bird and beast, wind, rain and snow – the total mountain. Slowly I have found my way in."[37] Or, as she puts it elsewhere, "I have walked out of the body and into the mountain. I am a manifestation of its total life."[38]

This journey of love with the mountain, in which she was forever moving from the outer to the inner landscape, back and forth, in and out, again and again, she saw essentially as pilgrimage. "It is a journey into Being," she says, "for as I penetrate more deeply into the mountain's life, I penetrate also into my own."[39] And although she speaks elsewhere of walking the flesh "transparent", she is not in any sense meaning a negation of her body or any aspect of herself.[40] She accesses the spiritual in and through her outward senses. Her body is like a portal into the unseen. "I am not out of myself," she writes, "but in myself. I am."[41]

Shepherd knew the Bible, including the story of the burning bush, well enough to also know the significance of the words I am. When Moses, as we have already noted, is described in the Book of Exodus encountering a bush that is on fire with divine presence without being consumed, he asks, "What is your name?" The response is not, "I am this or I am that. I am God or I am Lord." The response is "I am who I am" (Exod. 3:14). And in Hebrew the meaning of these words is not limited to the present tense alone. It can also mean "I have been who I have been" or "I will be who I will be". In other words, "Don't try to name me. Don't try to tame me with definition. Don't try to claim me as this or that. I am who I am. I transcend names. I am beyond designation."

The light that burns deep in all things, in the mountain, in Earth and all its life-forms, including every human being, is a light that cannot be captured by name or definition. And to be of this light, to be made by it and even composed of it, is to know that the heart of our being is ineffably sacred. There are many things that Shepherd would have delighted to be able to say about herself, that she was a woman, a teacher, a Scot, a daughter, a sister, a friend, a writer. But she knew also that none of these words captured her essence. Always she is more than what can be said, more than any designation or category or term of reference. What the mountain taught her, and what she comes to know in her journey of love with it, is that her essence, and the essence of every human being, is the essence also of Earth. "I am," she writes. "This is the final grace accorded from the mountain."[42] The journey into the heart of the natural world is a journey into reverence. It is a journey into seeing the I-am-ness of every life-form and every human being, and of never reducing the other to a category of being, whether that be of gender or religion, of race or nationality. I am who I am. And I will be who I will be. At the heart of my being is the light that has always been and that shines with uniqueness in each one of us and every life-form.

*

Shepherd writes at the beginning of *The Living Mountain* that what she is seeking is "to know the mountain's essential nature".[43] For it is in coming to know more of the mountain's essence that she comes to know more of her own essence and the essence of all life. She calls this knowing "a glow in the consciousness", a lighting up of inner awareness.[44] And she finds that it is in approaching the mountain with love that she moves most deeply into the heart of its nature and into the heart of her own nature.

In the Cairngorms, Shepherd is forever looking for the light that is the mountain's essence. Sometimes she glimpses it in its "fiercely pure" waters, as she describes them.[45] The rivers and mountain burns of the Scottish Highlands flow with such "elemental transparency," she says, that they can only actually be seen by their movement, the light of life glistening through them.[46] At other times it is through her sense of hearing that she catches something of the mountain's essential nature. In the high-pitched cry of a swift flying overhead, for instance, she hears "the free, wild spirit of the mountain".[47] Or, in birdsong at twilight, she listens to the sound of the infinite coming to her through the "small perishable throat" of a blackbird.[48]

But it is not just the *mountain's* essential nature that Shepherd is inviting us to know, it is the essence of *all* life. She calls it life "essentialised", when we become aware of the light deep within all life, the "enchanted radiance" at the heart of nature, the "infinitudes" that are all around us in earth, sea and sky, the "pure and subtle fire" that glows deep in the life of trees and brings them to bud in the spring.[49] This we can know not only in the natural world that surrounds us but also deep within the human mystery. We too shine. We are "irradiated" by an ever-living fire that burns deep in the core of our being.[50] Each one of us, she says, is a "unique and eternally intangible self."[51]

Intangible but, for Shepherd, always physical too. Experiences of the essence of life do not make the human body or the body of Earth "negligible", she says. "Flesh is not annihilated but fulfilled. One is not bodiless, but essential body."[52] Spirit and matter are one for Shepherd. The essence of our being is both physical and spiritual. As she writes in a poem entitled "The Hill", describing her experience of a landscape that shone with morning light, it was hard to tell if it was spirit or matter that she was witnessing, for "earth so mingled with heaven," she says, that they formed one reality not two.[53]

When we glimpse something of the eternally intangible in another human being, in their body and soul, or when the natural world becomes again a place of enchantment to us, alive with messages from the unseen, or when life is suddenly essentialized and we fleetingly see the light that is deep in all things, Shepherd calls these "moments of revelation".[54] They cannot be obtained "at will". We can't force them to happen. They are "unpredictable", she says, just as they are "unforgettable". They come to us as pure gift. Our role is simply to be alert and ready to receive them into ourselves. In such moments, she says, everything falls into perfect focus and, at last, one can read "the word that has been from the beginning".[55]

There can be little doubt that Shepherd knew the opening words of St. John's Gospel, "In the beginning was the Word ..." (John 1:1). She would have heard this verse read aloud many times in her life, not that she would have ever described herself as a particularly religious person. We know, however, that she attended church with her father every Sunday in the village of West Cults. It was a family tradition that she followed until her father's death in 1925, by which time she was thirty-two. And it had also been her mother's practice to attend church regularly until shortly after Shepherd's birth, when she suffered a mental breakdown that effectively kept her housebound for the rest of her long life. Shepherd knew not only the wild expanses of the mountain but the confined struggle of mental illness in her own home. But the family environment was a traditionally religious one, shaped by the strong scripture-devotion of the Free Kirk in Scotland. She, therefore, knew biblical imagery and used it in her writings, although never with a heavy hand. It is always with the fine subtlety of spirit and the delicate suggestiveness of tone that is true to the poetic.

The opening words of John's prologue, which speak of all things coming into being through the Word, provided Shepherd with a metaphor for pointing to the mountain's essence. It allowed her to poetically speak of everything as an utterance of the divine – every creature, every life-form, every human being, even every geological formation. They are all part of the great "annunciation of the Word", as she put it.[56] And it provided her with a way of summoning us to listen deeply and reverently to Earth. This is perhaps Shepherd's most prophetic offering to us for today, the invitation, indeed the imperative, to listen again to Earth that we may hear deep within it the source of our life and the hope of our well-being.

Although it is biblical imagery that Shepherd powerfully accesses at times, such as the burning bush that is not consumed or the word that has sounded from the beginning, she also accesses Eastern wisdom. Her notebooks indicate that early on she was reading the Indian writer Rabindranath Tagore. His Nobel Prize for Literature in 1913, awarded especially for his collection of poems entitled *Gitanjali* in which he addresses God as the Light within all life, had more widely opened the door for many in the Western world to India's sense of the sacred universe. Similarly, she had been attracted to the Theosophical vision of leading figures in Ireland's Celtic Twilight movement, like William Butler Yeats and George Russell, and their search within nature for the inner heart of all things. These influences helped shape Shepherd's use of biblical imagery and her own religious inheritance. They provided her with ways of seeing the human journey as essentially pilgrimage, travelling through the outer veil of reality into the inner light of being. And, in this, Shepherd anticipates one of the most prominent features of the Great Search of today, as we have seen, a willingness to learn from the wisdom of other traditions, allowing it to meet and mingle with the wisdom of our own spiritual inheritance.

But, for Shepherd, it is always particularly poetic utterance, whether explicitly religious or not, that most powerfully offers us glimpses into the "burning heart of all life".[57] She in fact uses the ancient church's definition of sacrament, "an outward and visible sign" of an inward and invisible reality, to express what poetic speech can do.[58] Words that are creatively spoken from deep within our relationship with Earth can give new expression to the light that is deep in all things and draw us back into true relationship with the heart of life. To her friend and fellow author Neil Gunn she says we need to find speech that will "irradiate the common" to bring us closer to the essence of life in every moment and encounter.[59] Let's have new ways of speaking, she says, "words not yet saturated with other people's meanings."[60] We need to find ways of speaking the world anew, using language that will release among us new ways of seeing and new ways of relating to Earth and one another. The word that has been from the beginning is a "life-giving word", says Shepherd, forever new.[61] Just as it is forever giving expression to new life in the body of Earth, so it can forever be spoken anew from within the human soul in ways that will awaken us again to wonder and reverence for Earth and all its life-forms. This, in so many ways, is exactly what Shepherd's *The Living Mountain* does. It opens our eyes to what she calls "pristine amazement" at life.

✻

"So I have found what I set out to find," she says in her concluding words of *The Living Mountain*, as she remembers her first sighting of the Cairngorms as a child from a hill on the edge of the range. "I could not contain myself. I jumped up and down. I laughed and shouted. There was the whole plateau, glittering white, within reach of my fingers, an immaculate vision, sun-struck, lifting against a sky of dazzling blue. I drank and drank. I have not yet done drinking that draught. From that hour I belonged to the Cairngorms."[62]

For the rest of her life, she did indeed belong to the Cairngorms, passionately in love with the mountain, and through her love affair with the mountain passionately in love with Earth. This is the love affair she invites us to be part of in our search for new beginnings. Her words lead us into fresh wonderment at the gift of life, and into deep gratitude for the sacredness of Earth. Inscribed on the Scottish five-pound note that celebrates the genius of Shepherd are words from a character in one of her novels, *The Quarry Wood*. They are spoken by a simple man of the earth, an Aberdeenshire farmer. "It is a grand thing to get leave to live," he says.[63] Shepherd knew the grandness of this gift and she helps reawaken us to it again and again in her writings.

In 1950 Shepherd wrote a poem from Achiltibuie in the mountainous northwest of Scotland, looking out over the Summer Isles and beyond them to the open sea:

> Here on the edge of Europe I stand on the edge of being.
> Floating on light, isle after isle takes wing.
> Burning blue are the peaks, rock that is older than thought,
> And the sea burns blue—or is it the air between? –
> They merge, they take one another upon them.
> I have fallen through time and found the enchanted world.
> Where all is beginning.
> The obstinate rocks
> Are a fire of blue, a pulse of power, a beat
> In energy, the sea dissolves
> And I too melt, am timeless, a pulse of light.[64]

Nan Shepherd was a unique pulse of light among us. For more than eighty years she shone as part of the glory of Earth. She died on February 27, 1981, returning to the ground from which she had come. But her words live on among us, helping us remember that we too are part of the shining radiance of Earth. Deep within us and all things is the enchanted world of light that is our beginning and our hope.

Shepherd was not an ecological activist. The age in which she lived was not yet conscious of the threat to Earth's well-being that is now calling into question the very future of humanity. But if she were alive today, I believe she would be bringing all her creative powers of utterance to help further awaken humanity to the urgent need for Earth's healing. If we allow her story to speak into our lives today, what we hear essentially is a story of love. She invites us again and again to fall in love with Earth. And it is love that will sustain the actions that this moment is urgently calling for if humanity and Earth are to be well, love for the "enchanted radiance" that is deep in all things.

MEDITATIVE PRACTICE: SEEKING EARTH

Nan Shepherd is a messenger to us of oneness with Earth. She invites us to know not just with our minds but with our bodies – to breathe in Earth's freshness, to listen to its silence and storms, to taste its juice in the crispness of an autumn apple, to see its colour in the new light of dawn and feel its wetness in the rain-washed landscape of grasses and trees around us. And in all of this to grow in passion for Earth as a lover for her beloved.

> *(pause to listen for what Shepherd's wisdom stirs in us)*

> As the body longs to waken to all its senses
> so my soul longs to know Earth again
> to breathe her in and touch her
> to taste her goodness and hear her song
> and forever to see fresh shinings of her life
> and seek her healing as my own.

> *(pause to be aware)*

> As the body longs to waken to all its senses
> so my soul longs to know Earth again.

Three

Seeking Presence: Martin Buber

It is the desire to ground spiritual wisdom in experience rather than in statements of faith. It is the conviction that the light of God shines in the body of Earth and in one another, and deep within us all, rather than limitedly within the walls and ministrations of religion. Martin Buber (1878–1965), one of the greatest Jewish teachers of the twentieth century, profoundly addresses this yearning in his writings. The world, he says, is "lit by eternity".[1] It is lit from within. The light of the divine can be looked for everywhere, in every moment, and deep within every encounter and relationship of life.

Many years ago, I met a Jewish man who had grown up in a Hasidic community in New York City. When he was young it had been his custom to go to a camp for Jewish boys every summer just up the Hudson River. He shared with me an experience from one of those summers that had changed his life. Word got around at the camp one day that the much-loved rabbi of their community, the Rebbe, as he was called, was visiting, and wanted to meet with the boys at the stream that ran through the centre of the camp. The boys rushed along the banks of the stream looking for the Rebbe. When they found him, he was standing in the flowing water, praying, rocking back and forth in that form of Hasidic prayer sometimes called "one-pointed concentration", seeking the presence of the divine at the heart of the moment.

The boys entered the stream to be with the Rebbe, and he said just one thing to them. "The water that we see flowing past us now will never flow past us again." He then returned into his rocking movement of prayer, and the boys joined him, swaying back and forth in mantric motion together. But the combination of the flowing waters and the rocking movement of prayer put the boy to sleep. When he woke up all the other boys were away, but the Rebbe, still standing and praying in the flowing water, was now steadying the boy with one arm around his back. This time the Rebbe didn't say anything to him but simply leaned forward and smiled into his eyes. In the rabbi's face the young boy glimpsed the countenance of the divine. This was a moment of grace that he cherished for the rest of his life. And it led him to be looking for the presence of God in every human face, in every life-form, and in every moment.

Encountering the presence of the divine is something that Buber invites us to be alert to in the whole of life. In his writings he describes such moments of encounter in his life from early boyhood onwards when he glimpsed the light of God in people, in creatures, and in the body of Earth. These experiences shaped his vision of reality.

Buber was born in Vienna of an Austrian Jewish family in 1878, and later lived and taught in Germany during the Nazi rise to power before fleeing to Jerusalem for safety in 1938. Although he wrote about encountering the divine in life, Buber preferred not to describe himself as a theologian for he was interested not in ideas *about* God but in our experiences *of* God. His focus was on the way we know sacred presence in one another and all things, or what he called our encounters with "the truly Present-One".[2]

Buber's most seminal work was entitled *I and Thou*. In it he speaks of two primary ways of being, or what he also calls our two main modes of relating in the world. The first, he says, is the "I-Thou" relationship.[3] This is when my depths, for instance, meet your depths, or when the open heart of one person encounters the open heart of another. It may be as simple and fleeting as when the eyes of two strangers meet and mingle briefly on a busy city street or as deep and enduring as the life-long intimacy of lovers. These encounters will sometimes be silent and still. At other times they will be accompanied by speech and action. And they can happen as readily as when two people stand together in conversation in a garden as when one person stands alone, listening to the sound of birdsong at twilight or unexpectedly seeing a sliver of crescent moon appear faintly in the early evening sky. But always, says Buber, when we encounter the Thou in another, whether that be in another person or in another life-form or in the radiance of sun, moon and stars, we are encountering "the eternal Thou".[4] We are experiencing the divine presence in and through the other.

The second primary mode of relating that Buber describes is what he calls the "I-It" relationship.[5] This is when something has become an object to us, a focus of our thought or action or intention. It is a way of relating when the other has ceased, at least for that moment, to be a living portal of presence to us. Instead, we are simply remembering or reflecting upon the other or making plans or working alongside the other. This, as we shall see, is for Buber neither good nor bad in and by itself. It depends on whether the balance is right and whether there is a true integration between these two ways of relating in which the I-It is allowed to serve the I-Thou at the heart of life.

The reality is that we are forever moving back and forth between I-Thou and I-It. After our eyes have briefly encountered those of a stranger on a street corner or after we have tasted love on the lips of another, we will very naturally move from these I-Thou moments into the realm of I-It. The other becomes an object of our thought. We may think, *Oh, her eyes sparkled with life* or *Her lips were beautifully moist*. In that moment the other has become a focus of our thought. We are not being immediately present to her so much as thinking about her. We have stepped away, however slightly, from the directness of encounter. And the other has become an It to us, or similarly a He or a She, an object of our thought. Or, equally naturally, after such I-Thou encounters, we may think *Oh, I had better hurry along to the shop now* or *I'd like to buy her some tulips*. In that moment we have moved from our encounter of presence into the world of action and getting things done. The reality, says Buber, is that we live in a "profoundly twofold" world, the realm of I-Thou and the realm of I-It.[6] They are not two worlds. They are one. And they need each other.

There is the Jewish story of paradise coming to a small village. The people become aware of the presence of the divine in one another and all things. They stand gazing enraptured at the colour and light of early dawn. They are so drawn by the presence of the divine in the nearby forest that they want to hug the trees in reverence. And they can't stop adoring the light of God in one another's eyes or singing and dancing with love, long into the night. But after two days and nights of paradise, they realize that nothing is getting done. No one is peeling the potatoes. No one is washing the dishes. The I-Thou relationship is at the heart of life, but without the I-It relationship, we cannot survive.

We are born with the Thou-instinct, says Buber, or what he calls "the instinct for communion".[7] At the heart of our being is the desire to be in true relationship. This is part of what it means to be made of the eternal Thou. It means that the sacred longing for interrelationship is an instinct deep within us. We see something of this in the newborn child. Buber describes how an infant, on hearing a kettle that has reached boiling point on the kitchen stove, will respond to the whistling sound by trying to make similar sounds in response. She wants "to give relation to the universe", he says.[8] This is why the child is so celebrated in most great spiritual traditions. "It is to such as these," as Jesus says, "that the kingdom of God belongs" (Matt. 19:14). The child's instinct for relationship is a manifestation of the sacred yearning for communion at the heart of all being.

Buber writes about his early boyhood encounters with a horse on his grandfather's farm. He would steal into the stable, unobserved, so that he could gently stroke the neck of the great dapple-grey stallion:

> What I experienced in touch with the animal was the Other, the immense otherness of the Other, which, however, did not remain strange ... but rather let me draw near and touch it. When I stroked the mighty mane, sometimes marvellously smooth-combed, at other times just as astonishingly wild, and felt the life beneath my hand, it was as though the element of vitality itself bordered on my skin, something that was not I ... and yet it let me approach, confided itself to me, placed itself elementally in relation of Thou to Thou with me.[9]

Buber remembers that even before beginning to pour oats into the bucket for the horse, it would gently raise its massive head to him, its ears flicking, and quietly snort as if in welcome. But there came a day when he became conscious of his hand stroking the neck of the mighty stallion and found himself thinking about how marvellous it felt to be touching the horse instead of simply being present to the horse. At that moment "something changed," he said, "it was no longer the same thing." The young Buber continued to visit the horse in the stable, but he had transitioned from the simple purity of the child's Thou-instinct into the ability also to reflect on his relationship with the horse. He had entered what, as we have seen, he calls the "profoundly twofold" nature of the world and our relationship with it which is neither I-Thou on its own, nor I-It. It is both.

A belief in the Thou-instinct at the heart of the child, and thus deep within every human being, is very different from the doctrine of original sin that has dominated so much Western Christian thought over the centuries. The latter has been used to give the impression, if not explicitly teach, that what is most original in us, or what is deepest in us, including the newborn child, is opposed to God rather than being of God. What has followed from this is the tragic assumption that what is deepest in every human being is not the Thou-instinct but the me-instinct, not the yearnings of the soul for relationship but the limited desires of the ego for self.

In contrast to this, Buber quotes a morning prayer that is used by faithful Jews throughout the world, "The soul which Thou hast given me [O God] is pure."[10] It is a prayer that celebrates the essential sacredness of the soul as opposed to the essential sinfulness of the soul. Our deep inner purity may have become infected or covered over in our lives. We may have fallen out of touch with the Thou-instinct that is deep within us, but it is there waiting to come forth again. Buber invites us to remember it at the heart of our being, to faithfully look for it deep in one another, and to be part of reawakening it in the world. This, for Buber, is the wellspring of our healing.

In the Christian tradition, it is important to remember that Jesus was a Jew, not a Christian. His teachings were based not on the doctrine of original sin as articulated by Imperial Christianity in the fourth century and following. His wisdom was rooted in Jewish thought and its celebration of the essential sacredness of the soul in every newborn child and in every human being waiting to come forth afresh.

The story of the burning bush in Hebrew scripture, in which, as we have seen, Moses encounters a bush that is on fire with divine presence without being consumed, is pivotal to Buber's way of seeing. The most significant stories of revelation, he believed, like this first story of divine self-disclosure in Hebrew tradition, point not to what is an exception in life but to what is at the heart of life, within every moment and every place. As my rabbi brother Nahum says, the important thing about this story is not that the bush is burning but that Moses noticed because every bush is burning. The whole universe is on fire with divine presence. We are being urged to notice!

When Moses becomes aware of the divine presence within the burning bush, he says that when he returns to his people and tells them that he has met the God of their ancestors, they will ask, "What is his name?" In response, God says to Moses, "I AM WHO I AM" (Exod. 3:14). These words in Hebrew are represented by the tetragrammaton YHWH, which in transliteration appears in some versions of scripture as Yahweh. But, to the faithful Jew, the name of God is never written or spoken, for God is beyond names. If one were to try to pronounce YHWH, however, it would simply sound like the exhalation of breath. The One, who is beyond names, is the Breath of life. Buber, as we have already noted, interprets YHWH to mean "the truly Present-One", or the One who is at the heart of every moment and everything that has being, the Breath of all life.

Moses's encounter with the burning bush is not about content. It is about presence. Moses doesn't come away from the experience with statements about God or with a name for God or a definition of the divine. Nor does he come away with divine prescriptions such as, "You must do this" or "You must believe that." "The guiding counsel of God," says Buber, "is simply the divine Presence communicating itself directly to the pure in heart." Revelation does not consist of the dispensing of religious commandments from above that are to be etched for ever into stone and followed meticulously. Rather, revelation consists of encounter, and "the Presence itself," says Buber, "acts as counsel."[11]

This was not well received unanimously by his Jewish contemporaries, especially the strict traditionalists of conservative Judaism who wanted to absolutize the commandments of their religion. They accused Buber of "religious anarchy" for his refusal to unquestioningly follow Jewish law.[12] Buber saw himself as a faithful son of Judaism, but for him the heart of his spiritual inheritance was not about religious law or doctrine. It was about faithfulness to the Presence that burns at the heart of all life.

Buber was respectful, however, toward those who chose to follow a stricter approach to Judaism. On one occasion in Manhattan, for instance, the Jewish Theological Seminary had organized a Sabbath meal in his honour. After the celebration he needed to get back to his hotel room fifty blocks from where they were gathering. It was ten o'clock at night, and a cold rain was falling. His hosts knew that Buber didn't mind riding in a car on the Sabbath, but this was not their practice, nor did they believe it was right to encourage another Jew to do so. Out of respect for the elderly Buber, however, and because the weather was bad, they offered to hail him a cab. But Buber responded, "No, I'll walk."[13] So, off he headed into the night with his hosts accompanying him in the cold rain. They walked together along Broadway for fifty blocks and arrived at the hotel, all soaking wet! But they had respected one another.

Buber may not have believed that our encounters with the living Presence translate directly into statements of faith or into religious laws to be strictly followed. He did believe, however, that encounters with the divine change us. Something new unfolds in our depths, he said. These moments of "supreme meeting", as he calls them, give rise to fresh light in our souls. It is "like the moon rising," he said, "in a clear starlit night."[14] Such moments cannot be preserved or absolutized as the definitive norm for others. They are simply to be "proved true" in our own lives, he said, by inspiring us to further seek the divine presence in one another and to be part of reawakening the world to the sacred fire that burns deep in all things.[15]

Buber distinguishes between "trust" and "belief", by which he means "trust in" and "belief that".[16] If I say to you, for instance, "I trust you," I am saying that I have faith in who you are and in the heart of your being. If, on the other hand, I say, "I believe such-and-such about you," I am saying that I have some information about you that I believe to be true, like your gender or name or home address. "Trust in," says Buber, derives from the Hebrew notion of *emunah*. "Belief that" is shaped by the Greek term *pistis*. What we hear in Jesus's teachings about the divine, says Buber, is the Hebrew notion of faith rather than the Greek understanding. "Trust in" is about giving ourselves to relationship with God, allowing the divine presence to be our inspiration and guide. "Belief that", on the other hand, consists of believing certain things to be true about God, like the name of the divine or the commandments of the divine, and placing our faith in adherence to such beliefs.

"How delicate are the appearances of the Thou," says Buber.[17] They come and go like the breeze on a summer evening. We don't know where the breeze comes from or where next it will be going. We simply open to it and are renewed by it. So it is with the delicate appearances of the divine in our lives. We are simply to open to them and find ourselves renewed. Buber calls this type of faith "holy insecurity".[18] Our encounters with the living Presence cannot be tied down or defined. We are simply to receive them as gifts and then let them pass in their own time like the summer breeze that will come again and renew us.

We cannot capture the mystery of the divine by time and place or by religious belief and utterance. God can be "addressed", says Buber, but can never be "expressed".[19] We can speak to God, uttering from the depths of our souls, but we can never truly speak about God. A German pastor once asked Buber if he believed in the divine. Buber responded by saying, "If to believe in God means to be able to talk about God in the third person, then I do not believe in God. But if to believe in God means to be able to talk to God, then I do believe in God."[20]

Humanity has been addressing the divine with many names since time immemorial. And Buber himself loved words and loved to use them in his prayers and writings. But he was always aware that words belong more to the realm of I-It than they do to the realm of I-Thou. We will always, however, want to use them, even in addressing the unnamable One. For it is the way a lover longs for language to speak into the heart of the beloved. And when we do use names to address God faithfully, they are hallowed by love. In other words, we use them to serve our encounter with the eternal Thou. Just as Jesus prays, "Our Father in heaven, *hallowed* be thy name ..." (Matt. 6:9), so we can say

"Our Father," "Our Mother," "Our Light," "Our Maker" while also saying "but hallowed be your name," that is, "no name can ever capture thee." It is a way of remembering that, although we are using words to address the divine, God is always more than anything that can be said. Every word we use about God is a metaphor, says Buber. With one exception. The word *Thou*. For when we use the word *Thou* in prayer, we are speaking *to* the divine, not *about* the divine.

It is sometimes argued that the word *God* should be dropped from our religious vocabulary. It is so overused that it has become like a proper name for the divine. And we forget that the source of the mystery is beyond names. Buber wrestled with this matter, notably in his relationship with Paul Tillich. As a young man he attended a talk given by the great German American theologian in which Tillich argued that we must abandon the word *God* because it has been so linked to notions of transcendence in ways that have diminished our sense of the immanence or within-ness of the divine. At the end of the talk Buber stood up in the lecture hall and said that we must not do away with the word *God* because it is, as he put it, "a primordial word".[21] It comes from deep within the history of the human soul, preceding even the advent of religion. Therefore, it must be kept. Many years later, Tillich shifted in his opinion. Buber "was right," he said. The word *God* links us to the earliest strands of spiritual awareness, so, let us keep it. But let us also forge new metaphors to use for this moment in time, as Tillich did so creatively in speaking of the divine as the "Ground of Being".

One of the implications of saying that words for the divine need to be hallowed is to remember that this is how we should address the heart of one another as well. Each one of us is made of the divine, as is every creature and life-form. The essence of the other, therefore, can never be captured by name or definition, such as nationality or gender or race or religion. The other is always essentially "Thou".

✸

Some years ago, I was on a plane flying into Atlanta to give an evening talk on Buber's *I and Thou*. Sitting beside me on the flight was a young Indian woman with a veil partly covering her face. Only her beautiful eyes were showing. We said a brief hello before I turned to look over my notes for the evening presentation. But during takeoff I fell fast asleep. When I woke, the young woman gently tapped me on my arm and pointed to the notes on my lap. "What does 'I am who I am' mean?," she asked.

By now she was unveiled, so I was able to see the full beauty of her countenance. I said to her, "You are a woman, you are Indian, you are a daughter, and I think you are Hindu." To which she nodded. "But none of these words capture the heart of your being. You are always more than anything that can be said." She then told me a little about herself and about her long journey from India, and that her name was Pushpa. But as she spoke her eyes began to fill with tears, and she asked, "Who am I? My parents tell me who I am. And my religion tells me who I am, as does my culture, but who am I?" She then explained to me that this was her first trip to America and that she was travelling to meet her husband, who was still something of a stranger to her. The wedding, an arranged marriage, had happened recently in India. She was now coming to take up residence with him and his family in a strange land. And she was frightened.

On hearing her story, I pointed to another word in my notes, the word *Thou*. And I said to her, "If I were to try to speak into the heart of your being, this is the word I would use, 'Thou'. I would use it to speak to that part of you that cannot be named, that part of you that is divine and forever free." She paused, then said in response, "Thank you. Your words are helpful. I feel less afraid." Toward the end of the flight, I said, "Pushpa, tomorrow morning when I pray at the rising of the sun, I will pray for you and for new beginnings for you in this country." In response she gazed directly into my eyes and said, "And I pray for you."

On arrival in Atlanta, I realized it probably wouldn't be a good idea to be seen by Pushpa's new American family walking through the arrivals gate with her, so we said our farewells on the plane and exchanged blessings. In the terminal, however, at baggage claim, I looked across the carousel and there was Pushpa surrounded by her Atlanta family. She too was looking across the carousel in the opposite direction and our eyes met. We didn't nod or gesture. There was only the slightest of smiles between us. But in her eyes, I glimpsed the light of the eternal Thou. And I left the airport that day knowing that I too had been truly seen.

"Everything is waiting to be hallowed," says Buber. Everything and everyone is yearning to be truly seen and reverenced.[22] This is what happens in the I-Thou encounter. And we are changed by it. It takes us closer to the heart of our being again and to the heart of one another, made of God.

In 1899 Buber met his wife, Paula Winkler, a brilliant university student who later became a well-known novelist. She was from an aristocratic Catholic family in Munich. When they met it was as if they had known each other from the beginning of time. "When I found you," he later said to her, "I found my soul. You came and gave me my soul."[23] This gift, however, the finding of his soul through Paula, came at great cost to her. Paula's family rejected her because of her relationship with Buber. They lived together and had two children, Rafael and Eva, before she eventually converted to Judaism. They were formally married in 1907.

Sometimes an I-Thou encounter changes our life, as it did for Buber and his wife. At other times it is brief and passing, like my encounter with Pushpa. But always it carries blessing with it and always it comes as pure grace. It is not created by us, says Buber, but by attentively "waiting" and being ready to receive the gift when it comes.[24] We cannot produce I-Thou encounters, but we can prepare ourselves spiritually, through meditation, silence and prayer, to be more open and ready to receive these encounters when they are given. And the only time and place to receive the gift of meeting the divine in one another is here and now, by being present to every moment and every encounter of life. It can be called the Now of Thou.

∗

How do we live in the now, alive to the eternal Presence in one another and every life-form, especially when the realm of I-It gains prominence in our lives and world?

Buber quotes the Talmud, the central text of Rabbinic Judaism, as saying that there is both the "good urge" and the "evil urge" deep within us.[25] The good urge, he says, enables us to be ready to receive I-Thou encounters in our lives. The evil urge, on the other hand, drives us toward the It. This is not to say that the realm of I-It is evil in and by itself. As we have already noted, we need the realm of I-It to survive. The problem comes when I-It gains "mastery" over us and "overruns" our Thou-urge.[26]

Buber speaks of good and evil as the "yes-position" to life and the "no-position".[27] When we begin to be dominated by the realm of I-It we are in danger of saying no to the heart of life or of missing the divine presence deep within one another and the body of Earth. "Sin is lurking at the door," as the Book of Genesis says, "and its desire is for you, but you must master it" (Gen. 4:7). In every moment of life, in every encounter and relationship, the no-position is present and ready to assert itself. But the yes-position is also there. The eternal Thou is beckoning to us from the heart of every moment, both individually and collectively, and especially during times of conflict and war, when the realm of I-It becomes "gigantically swollen" and threatens to overpower us.[28]

Buber was no stranger to the ways in which awareness of the presence of the divine in another can be neglected or lost sight of. At the age of three, his mother disappeared. Many years later it was discovered that she had secretly fled to Russia to marry another man. Suddenly as a young boy he had been denied the presence of perhaps the most important bearer of I-Thou relationship in his life. Then as an adult, during his professorship at the University of Frankfurt, he witnessed the Nazi rise to power in Germany and the silencing of Jewish academics and the denial of public education for Jews, early signs of what was eventually to be known as the "Final Solution", the Nazi policy of systematic genocide of the Jewish people. He witnessed his people being viewed and treated as "It", as a so-called "problem" to be got rid of.

Buber early on was part of leading the spiritual resistance to Nazi domination in Germany. He became a fearless spokesman for his people. When Jews were denied public education in 1933, he founded the Central Office for Jewish Adult Education to try to ensure the ongoing education of Jews in his country. He also played a leading role in Jewish-Christian dialogue during these years in Germany, to nurture a deeper understanding and relationship between faiths. Such was his stature of leadership among German Jews that the Nazis referred to him as the "arch-Jew".[29] They banned him from public speech in 1935 and ransacked his house in Heppenheim. In 1938 Buber, fearing for his family's safety, fled the country with his wife and children to find sanctuary in Jerusalem.

But in Jerusalem he witnessed Jews perpetrating on the Arab population of Palestine some of the same wrongs that were being done to his own people in Europe. He courageously spoke out against this too. "The people who come to Zion under a holy banner," he said, "have become criminals."[30] He saw that many of his Jewish brothers and sisters were blind to the presence of God in the Arab population, and he lamented the way violence was being used by them to create nationhood. In the following years of conflict in Palestine, he asked how is it that otherwise good and loving people have come to believe that "brother-murder will prepare the way for brotherhood".[31] Buber described these years in Europe and the Middle East not as the "death of God", as the German philosopher Friedrich Nietzsche did before him in Europe, but as the "eclipse of God", human beings and even whole nations becoming blind to the presence of the divine in each other.[32] And, of the three wars that he witnessed in his lifetime, World War I, World War II, and the war in Palestine, it was the last, he said, that for him was "the most grievous", for he had seen his own people treating another people as "It" rather than looking for the eternal "Thou" in them.[33]

But never did Buber lose faith in the possibility of transformation. The Thou-urge in us can never be erased, he said, and no matter how far things have gone awry, "the buried relational power" in us can rise again.[34] Redemption, or what he also called "the restoration of betweenness", is about returning to true relationship.[35] It is about the heart of our being, even the heart of a whole people, "turning" again to the heart of the other.[36] Maybe this is the defining posture of the Great Search today, to commit ourselves to turning again to the sacred essence of one another and Earth. It is this that will enable a true restoration of betweenness.

After the Second World War, Buber was nominated for the annual Peace Prize by the Frankfurt Book Fair in Germany. He chose to accept the award even though he was viciously attacked for doing so by the Israeli press and by Jewish newspapers around the world. In their eyes Germany was simply to be condemned, not to be related to as a nation that could change. But Buber believed that no one should be considered "absolutely unredeemable".[37] "Everyone sins," he said, "but everyone may turn back."[38] "The gates are never closed," as the Midrashic text in Psalms 65 puts it, or, as Jesus says, "Knock, and the door will be opened for you" (Matt. 7:7). Always there remains the possibility of turning and of new beginnings.

Buber continued to be part of dialogue in Germany between Jews and Christians after World War II. He saw clearly, however, that the Church needed to give up its claims of superiority if there was to be true relationship. But Buber brought to this dialogue a profound respect for Jesus as "the son of our people", as he called him.[39] "From my youth onwards, I have found in Jesus my great brother," he wrote in 1951. "My own fraternally open relationship with him has grown ever stronger and clearer, and today … I am more than ever certain that a great place belongs to him in Israel's faith and that this place cannot be described by any of the usual categories."[40] Especially, it was Jesus's words about love for the enemy that deeply spoke to Buber. This is a teaching, he said, that derives its light from the world of Judaism but "outshines it".[41] As early as *I and Thou* he had described Jesus as illustrating the way of true relationship with the divine. But this was not to see Jesus as an exception to humanity. It was to see him rather as a revelation of the true depths of each one of us. As Buber later put it, "I do not believe *in* Jesus … I believe *with* Jesus."[42] Just as he worked to restore true relationship with Germany, as well as with Christianity, so in Palestine he gave himself tirelessly to reconciliation between Jews and Arabs. In 1939 he was part of founding the League for Jewish-Arab Rapprochement and Cooperation. He believed that a binational state could be formed, not the partition that eventually was declared between Israel and Palestine and that paved the way for many of the deep wrongs that are being done by the state of Israel to the people of Palestine today.

Buber was committed to the well-being of his people, but always he worked for the well-being of all people, or what he called "national universalism".[43] By this he meant a nationhood that would serve the well-being of the entire world, not just one's own nation. The renewal of Judaism and the renewal of humanity were for Buber two sides of the same coin. "Our soul's deepest humanity and our soul's deepest Judaism mean and will the same thing," he said.[44] It is the whole of humanity, not just the dispersed men and women of Israel, that need to be gathered again in relationship. Every nation, every race and every religion are part of the scattered diaspora of humanity, needing to be restored to oneness again.

Buber died at his home in Jerusalem on June 13, 1965. The prime minister of Israel, Levi Eshkol, said that Buber in his life and teachings had revealed to the world "the soul of Judaism".[45] To Buber that would have meant revealing to the world a belief in the light of the divine at the heart of every moment and deep within every person and life-form.

He believed that what each of us can do in this world is to "struggle to move it just one inch in the right direction", and if we succeed in this, he added, we have done much.[46] Buber might be described as having shifted the world many inches in the right direction. His vision of the light that can be looked for in every situation and every encounter has touched the lives of countless numbers of men and women across the world in disciplines as varied as education, ecology, politics and theology.

Part of what he inspires in us is a sense of hope for the present moment. Despite what we have done to one another and to Earth, whether individually or collectively, newness is forever trying to rise within us and among us. In every hour, he said, what has never been before comes into the world as "ten thousand new countenances".[47] And every situation, like the face of every newborn child, is calling us back into true relationship. It calls for "presence", he said. "It demands you."[48] For it is presence that is the greatest gift we can offer one another. And presence is the greatest gift we can receive. Here and now, the gift of presence coming to us through one another and through Earth.

MEDITATIVE PRACTICE: SEEKING PRESENCE

Martin Buber is a messenger of presence to us. He invites us to be alive to God in one another and in every manifestation of life, and to know that now is the time of divine presence, always now – within us, around us, and between us – and to open our hearts to each moment, looking always for the gift of presence that calls us back to our true selves.

> *(pause to listen for what Buber's wisdom stirs in us)*

> As thirst longs to be quenched
> so my soul longs to drink again
> at the fount of eternal presence
> everywhere
> rising from the wellspring of life
> gracing the countenance of a stranger
> deep in the soil of Earth
> and growing from the ground like a bush on fire.

> *(pause to be aware)*

> As thirst longs to be quenched
> so my soul longs to drink again
> at the fount of eternal presence
> everywhere.

PART TWO

Four

Seeking Awareness: Carl Jung

Carl Gustav Jung (1875–1961), the founder of analytical psychology, said that humanity's "worst sin" is lack of awareness, or "unconsciousness", as he termed it.[1] When we are unaware of what is happening within us, or oblivious to what is occurring around us, we are more likely to stumble in the dark than walk in the light. We are prone to confusion. This is as true of us individually as it is together. What are the things we need to be more aware of in our lives and world, in relation to Earth and one another as nations and races, and in our own inner depths as individuals? No matter how uncomfortable it may be to grow in awareness, nor how challenging and even painful, Jung calls us into greater and greater consciousness. The journey into wholeness will not happen without it.

Despite our frequent lack of awareness, including our capacity to deny reality, deep within us is an instinct for consciousness. "Within the soul," said Jung, "from its primordial beginnings there has been a desire for light."[2] Not only physical light but spiritual light, a desire to see, both inwardly and outwardly.

Religion in its origins was an attempt to address this longing for awareness. Jung questions, however, whether our religious traditions have penetrated deeply enough beneath the surface. Many of us today share Jung's doubt. Is our desire for light being sufficiently nurtured by religion as we know it? If not, how do we more fully access the yearnings of the Spirit within us? And how can our religious traditions more deeply serve these yearnings?

Jung is a messenger to us of the healing energies of consciousness.

By training and profession, he was a psychoanalyst, delving into the depths of the "psyche", a term that is derived from the Greek word *psukhe*, which means "soul". He can be described most simply, therefore, as a doctor of the soul seeking to bring wholeness and healing to human life by accessing the longings for light that are within us. He calls us to grow in awareness, both individually and together, no matter where it takes us, in the confidence that awareness is essential on the pathway to truth.

For Jung the inner world of the soul is as boundless as the outer world of the universe in its vast stretches of light and dark that reach endlessly through time and space. The human soul is like a microcosm of the macrocosm, an inner universe that corresponds to the infinity of the outward universe. Jung begins his autobiographical work *Memories, Dreams, Reflections* by quoting the nineteenth-century poet Samuel Taylor Coleridge, who said that a person who is seeking awareness of the human soul is like an astronomer exploring the heavens. "He looked at his own Soul with a Telescope," wrote Coleridge. "What seemed all irregular, he saw and shewed to be beautiful Constellations; and he added to the Consciousness hidden worlds within worlds."[3]

For Jung there are hidden worlds within the world of the soul. And at the heart of it all is the "valley of diamonds", as he called it, a place of immortal shining of light through which we have all passed in our journey of birth into this world.[4] This is not to romanticize life. "The world into which we are born is brutal and cruel," he wrote, yet at the same time it is full of "divine beauty".[5] Awareness of both the light and the dark, the brutality of life as well as its beauty, is vital to our healing. It helps reconnect us to the true heart of our being.

Jung uses the word soul, but he is wary of religion's attempts to pin the word down with precision and limit it only to the human species. The soul is not only the breath of human life. It is the breath of all life, the *anima mundi*, the animating life force of the universe. It is the vital spark in all things, distinct but not separate from our physicalness. The light of the soul can be glimpsed in one another's eyes and in the vitality of every life-form. It is a "glancing, Aeolian thing," he said, "elusive as a butterfly."[6] We cannot define it, but we can know its stirrings and motions within us and in everything that has life.

Christianity speaks about human beings having an immortal soul, but, as Jung said, it generally "has very few kind words" to say about the soul.[7] In most Western Christian thought, the soul has been described as sinful and ignorant rather than beautiful and sparkling with light. But for Jung our "true quintessence" is the *imago Dei*, the eternal likeness of the divine within us.[8] In his professional writings as a psychologist, he refers to this as the "God-Image" deep in every person. In his autobiography, however, toward the end of his life, when he is showing himself more openly to the world, Jung refers to our essence simply as "God".[9] "Like every other being," he says, "I am a splinter of the infinite deity."[10] We come from the divine. And at the core of our being we shine, like the translucence of jewels in sunlight. The great challenge for religion today is to return to the realm of enabling an experiential knowledge of the divine within us and among us rather than simply instilling an acceptance of creedal statements about the divine. The direct and immediate encounter of God in the body of Earth and one another, and deep within our own souls, is at the inception of all great religion. The problem is that these original experiences of the divine that gave rise to our religious traditions have "stiffened into mere objects of belief," said Jung, rather than being viewed as expressions of how we can continue to know the divine.[11] "The bridge from dogma to the inner experience of the individual has broken down," he said.[12]

Jung tells the story of one of his clients, a Swiss theologian, who dreamed that he was standing on the slope of a mountain looking out over a beautiful valley covered in dense forest. In the dream the theologian knew there was a lake in the middle of the woods, but he had never visited it before. Now, however, he was determined to reach the waters. As he approached the lake, the atmosphere grew mysterious, and suddenly "a light gust of wind passed over the surface of the water".[13] And he woke with a cry of terror.

Jung believed that the wind that passed over the surface of the waters in the dream was the Spirit that blows where it wills. It was this that terrified the dreamer, an immediate experience of the divine. For the theologian, the Spirit was something to be read about in the Bible or religiously adhered to in religious creeds. It was not a living mystery to be encountered in the depths of one's own being. The experience of the presence of the divine moving over the waters of his soul was terrifying for the theologian. Where did it come from and where was it going? So, instead of the forest being enchanted, it became a haunted woods, and he was seized with terror. Sometimes we fear the immediacy of the divine. It becomes entirely a *mysterium tremendum* (a mystery that frightens), as the writer Rudolf Otto named it, rather than also a *mysterium fascinosum* (a mystery that attracts).[14]

In 1882 when Nietzsche said, "God is dead ... we have killed him," he was not making a comment about the existence, or nonexistence, of God.[15] Rather, he was indicating that our experience of the divine has died. Similarly, Jung said that "the present is a time of God's death and disappearance."[16] By this he meant that religion has become focused on doctrines *about* the divine rather than experiences *of* the divine. Deep in our souls, however, there is a longing for the Spirit, not by proxy but by direct experience. It is a yearning for life's immediacy, both spiritually and physically, like "the warm red blood pulsating" within our veins, said Jung.[17]

The death and disappearance of God, as Jung put it, has led to the modern decline of religion. When he was a boy, only twelve years of age, Jung had a prophetic intuition of the coming collapse of Western Christianity. Walking home from school one day, as he passed through the cathedral square of Basel, he became aware of an image that so shocked him that he hid it away in his unconscious for decades, until finally in his sixties he was able to look at it again and speak about it. What he saw within himself that day as a schoolboy in the cathedral square of Basel was God sitting on a golden throne high above the world, and from under the throne an "enormous turd" fell, crashing through the sparkling new roof of the cathedral, shattering it to pieces and breaking the walls asunder.[18]

We are living in the midst of the great turd falling. And it is not just falling. It has already smashed into the edifice of Western Christianity, and the walls of religion are crumbling. As Jung later wrote, "God refuses to abide by traditions, no matter how sacred."[19] If religion fails to enable a direct experience of the divine, depending instead solely on the testimony of great teachers and prophets of the past, it will collapse. If it is not pulsating with the warm red blood of experience and a fresh awareness of the living presence of the Spirit within us and among us, it serves no useful purpose for the well-being of humanity and Earth today.

Carl Jung was born in the Swiss town of Kesswil on the shores of Lake Constance, but he spent most of his boyhood farther along the Rhine in the city of Basel, the cultural capital of Switzerland. There his father, Paul Jung, was a Swiss Reformed pastor, upright and orthodox, living in accordance with the doctrines of the church. His mother, on the other hand, Emilie Preiswerk, was a woman of "hearty animal warmth", as Jung described her.[20] Although she outwardly conformed to the teachings and practices of Swiss Reformed Christianity, there was another side to her that shone with the wisdom of the natural world. She was like "a priestess in a bear's cave," said Jung.[21] She knew things that were not simply derived from books and common opinion but from a deeper source within herself. The relationship between mother and father was a marriage of opposites. His father was like the theologian terrified by dreaming of the Spirit that swept as a wind over the waters. Religion for Paul Jung was about consent to propositional statements about God rather than about direct experience of the untamed Spirit that blows where it wills. His mother, on the other hand, had a mind in tune with natural sources. It welled up from Earth, said Jung, like a natural spring and brought with it intuitive wisdom. Jung witnessed in his parents two different types of knowing, one guided by reason and intellect, the other by intuition and feeling. His father's way of knowing often frustrated him as a young man, confined as it was to the mind. His mother's way of knowing had at times frightened him as a boy, issuing forth from some hidden source within her. In time Jung's path of knowledge brought both reason and intuition, the intellect and feeling, into a creative unity of knowing.

Our journey into awareness needs both these ways, the head as well as the heart, reason as well as intuition. And part of what we are being invited to be aware of comes to us through our parents and the long descent of ancestors through whom we have come into being. Our inheritance is both physical and spiritual. Just as the body has a physical prehistory of millions of years, so it is with the soul. The past lives in us, "in our very blood," he said.[22] The practice of awareness, therefore, takes us deep into our own history.

Jung had a dream that opened him to a greater awareness of the layers of inheritance that he carried within himself from the past. In the dream, he was in the upper storey of a house which he did not recognize but knew to be his own. There were precious old paintings on the wall that intrigued him. It then occurred to him that he didn't know anything about the lower floor of the house, so he descended the stairs to the ground level. There everything was much older and darker, and he realized it probably dated to the fifteenth or sixteenth century. As he wandered from room to room, he began to think, *Now I really must explore the whole house!* He came upon a heavy door and opened it. Beyond the door he discovered a stone stairway that led down into a cellar. Descending again, he found himself in a beautifully vaulted room that looked ancient. Examining the walls, he discovered layers of brick among the ordinary stone blocks, and realized the room dated to Roman times. His interest by now was fully aroused. He looked more closely at the stone slabs on the floor, and in one of these he discovered a ring. When he pulled it, the stone slab lifted, and again he saw another stairway of narrow steps leading farther and farther into the depths. These too he descended and came to a low cave cut into the rock. Thick dust lay on the floor, and in the dust were scattered bones and broken pottery, like the remains of a primitive culture. Also on the floor were two human skulls, very old and half disintegrated. Then he awoke.[23]

We carry the past within us, both the immediate past of our families and the distant past of our species. Awareness leads us into both the conscious and unconscious dimensions of our being. It invites us to be alert to what we have already known and experienced in our lives, as well as to what we don't yet know and the immense history that flows through us unconsciously from those who have gone before. Intuition, said Jung, is perception through our unconscious depths whereas reason is perception through the conscious mind. Our conscious side is but the tip of an iceberg. Most of who we are is hidden in the waters of the unconscious. True self-knowledge, therefore, is not just about our conscious self. It includes paying attention to our unknown depths which come to us most readily through intuition and dreams and the imagination. These depths arise from within us not on demand but by their own prompting. They come as pure gift. Our role is simply to be ready to receive them into our conscious self and translate them in our lives into action and relationship.

Awareness that comes to us via the unconscious can be described as "moon-like", says Jung.[24] Awareness via the conscious mind, on the other hand, is sun-like. We need both. The moon's white radiance in the dark night sky invites us to be aware of the mystery that we are part of and the essential oneness of everything around us. The hard edges of day are softened, and we are more aware of the interrelationship of all things than the distinctness of each thing. When we walk under the sun's light, on the other hand, we are more attentive to the uniqueness of each part. Moon-like awareness and sun-like awareness are given to complete each other. Our task is to be attentive to what the Spirit is bringing to our awareness, whether through the conscious or the unconscious within us, and to remain alert to both the light and the shadow, the beauty and the brokenness that exist within us individually and among us collectively.

Years ago, I had a dream in which I was trying to sneak into Jung's personal study at the top of his Bollingen Tower on the shores of Lake Zurich. It was for him a place of solitude into which he invited very few people. I thought he wasn't in, so I was ascending a spiral staircase which, in the dream, was on the outside of the building rather than the inside. Suddenly Jung popped his head out of the study window above me and said in his heavily accented English, "Come up." When I reached the top of the stairs, I found that we weren't in fact in the study but on the flat roof of the tower from which we could see in every direction. We then began to take turns playing an ancient instrument that was like a precursor of the French horn. Our intention was to sound the lowest note possible. At one point I was standing behind Jung, massaging his neck and shoulders, thinking that, if I could relax him, he would manage to sound the lowest note. Sure enough, it came, a long deep sound that issued forth as if from the beginning of time.

In response to the sounding of the note, people came out of the woods from the four directions carrying rolled-up animal hides that they placed on the ground in front of us. They then unfurled the hides, and within them we could see the remains of human beings who had died centuries, even millennia, earlier. The skeletons all bore the marks of violence, axe blows to the head, spear thrusts to the ribs, signs of the woundedness and brokenness that come down to us from the past in our families and cultures and nations.

Awareness, importantly, is not just about the light that is within us. The Spirit is inviting us to know also the pain and suffering, the wrong and violence that we carry deep in the memory of our bodies and souls. Awareness of both is essential in our journey toward wholeness.

The part to be played by religion in all this is immense, reconnecting us to what has been torn apart, the conscious from the unconscious, the rational mind from the intuitive, the West from the East, humanity from Earth. For, in essence, religion is about "the completeness of life," said Jung, "a life which contains both sides."[25] Religion evolved originally to hold life together, Heaven and Earth, spirit and matter, the head and the heart, the physical and the spiritual. The origins of the word *religion* speak of its purpose. It is derived from the Latin *religare*, which means to bind back together. It is this that our religious traditions urgently need to do again, to open our awareness to both the outer and inner world, the known and the unknown, the past and the present, the seen and the unseen, all of which exist within us and among us as individuals and together.

※

In 1907 Jung met Sigmund Freud, the founder of psychoanalysis. It was to be a relationship of great significance for both men even though it eventually ended in painful disagreement about the nature of the human soul. Jung was almost twenty years Freud's junior, and still a young man when the relationship began. Their first meeting in Vienna was one of deep mutual attraction and engagement, resulting in a conversation that lasted thirteen hours! What followed were six years of intense correspondence and collaboration. Freud even came to see Jung as his adopted son and successor.

The differences that eventually emerged between them, however, were significant. Freud believed that the human soul is most deeply characterized by the sex drive and an instinct for aggression. Jung, on the other hand, came to see our essence as spiritual. Our sexual yearnings, therefore, are part of the God-Image within us, expressions of a sacred desire for oneness and interrelationship. To put it theologically, Freud was speaking the language of original sin. Jung, on the other hand, was speaking the language of original blessing.

Freud refused to consider Jung's developing ideas about the human soul and formally broke with him in 1913, as did most of the psychoanalytical world at the time. Jung was left virtually alone in the professional world of psychology. In the same year he suffered a psychotic breakdown and entered a time of isolation for nearly six years. The personal cost of his rupture with Freud was huge. But it was also a defining moment in his journey. As he later wrote, "Only the wounded physician heals."[26] Only to the extent that we know our own brokenness can we help minister wholeness to others. In the end, Jung's own woundedness played an enormous part in enabling him to be a bearer of healing in the world.

Around the same time as his personal breakdown, he became aware of a foreboding collapse among the European world of nations. As he later described it, "In October [1913], while I was alone on a journey, I was suddenly seized by an overpowering vision: I saw a monstrous flood covering all the northern and low-lying lands between the North Sea and the Alps … I realized that a frightful catastrophe was in progress. I saw the mighty yellow waves, the floating rubble of civilization, and the drowned bodies of uncounted thousands. Then the whole sea turned to blood."[27]

The vision recurred over the next number of weeks, and in the spring of 1914 a similar dream came to him three times. In August of that year, World War I began. The sea of blood was becoming a reality. Jung now saw more clearly than ever what his task in life was to be. He was to try to understand the relationship between inner well-being and outward well-being. For the outer world and the inner world are not two separate worlds. They are one. And the way we seek wholeness within us as individuals relates also to the way we are to seek wholeness together. They both need the Spirit's healing energies of awareness.

During these years of personal struggle and growth, and afterward in his work with clients, Jung used mandalas, in addition to dreams and active imagination, as a tool of awareness. The Sanskrit word *mandala* means circle. They appear in all the great spiritual traditions of humanity, ranging from Buddhist sand mandalas in the East to rose windows in the Christian cathedrals of the West, as well as the medicine wheels of Native American tribes and the bora mandalas of indigenous Australians. Jung saw that the circle represents a striving for wholeness. It is a symbol of the oneness of the universe in which so-called opposites are held together, the sun and the moon, light and dark, the masculine and the feminine, East and West. Everything belongs within the circle. Our challenge is to become aware of the interrelationship of all things, and how opposites are given to complete each other. He described the mandala as a refuge of inner reconciliation and wholeness. In working with mandalas, he was seeking to know the relationship between the things that divide us, both within ourselves individually as well as collectively in the world. It was a way of seeking reintegration and balance.

The problem of "the union of opposites," said Jung, is at the heart of our collective struggles in the world as well as our personal journeys.[28] The more inattentive we are to bringing opposites back into relationship, "the more the devil drives" us on, he said.[29] We tear apart what belongs together. Nothing exists without its opposite, said Jung. The life of one species or one nation relates to the life of every species and every nation, even those that may seem entirely different to us. Failure to integrate so-called opposites in our lives and world, said Jung, leads to "a painful fragmentariness" in life and a ripping apart of Earth's essential oneness.[30]

We remain unintegrated when we refuse the meeting and mingling of opposites within us. This is as true collectively as it is individually.

The deepest energies of our being are given to find wholeness in relationship to all things, not in isolation. And for Jung the "supreme pair of opposites" is the combination of masculine and feminine energies that run through us all.[31] By this he did not simply mean the relationship between men and women, or male and female. He meant the marriage of opposites within us that express themselves distinctly as masculine on the one hand and feminine on the other. They are not dualities, he said, they are polarities, joined by a continuous spectrum of life's deepest energies flowing through us and through the body of Earth. And they find their completion in oneness, not in separation. This is why true sexual union is an "experience of the divine," says Jung.[32] It is not merely an expression of libido energies driven by the desire for self-satisfaction, as Freud argued. It is a deep longing of the Spirit in the human soul for the oneness from which we and all things have come.

Part of the marriage of opposites relates also to the relationship between good and evil in our lives and world. Jung more and more came to see that the roots of both good and evil are found in all of us. During times of conflict and war, for instance, we are to look for goodness in our so-called enemy as well as in ourselves. Similarly, we are to be alert to the presence of evil within us, and in our own people and our own nation, as well as in those who are opposed to us. If we are to truly engage with the problem of evil, said Jung, and be part of reconciliation in the world, we must first confront the falseness in our own souls before we look for it in our enemies. We will find good and evil, light and darkness, love and hatred, within us as well as beyond us.

This again is where the true heart of religion can strengthen us in the journey. And, as Jung makes clear, it is a journey into wholeness, not a journey into "perfection".[33] It is not a matter of perfectly conforming to some outward standard of religious belief and behaviour. It is a matter of opening to the Spirit's yearning for integration in the depths of our being, and then bringing the heart of who we are into true relationship with the heart of one another and Earth.

The greatest obstacle to the work of wholeness in our lives is the shadow side of our ego when it tries to be lord of the manor, as it were, in charge of the whole house of our being instead of simply a servant to the soul in the domestic quarters of our life. The ego is forever trying to make things easy for itself rather than serving true relationship in our lives and world. We need to "celebrate a Last Supper" with our ego, says Jung.[34] Not just once but again and again. We need to die to the separating energies of the ego that we may live from our true depths in union with the divine in Earth and one another. This is where religion can serve us if we will allow it again to enable the essential work of self-giving for the sake of wholeness. Jung reminds us that the word *sacrifice* is derived from the Latin *sacrificare*, which means to make holy or to make whole. Religion in its truest expressions, including spiritual practice and discipline, is about making us whole again by freeing us from imprisonment to the ego, whether that be the individual ego of our personhood or the collective ego of our nation or race or species.

This is not to put down the ego which is our sacred faculty of consciousness and willpower. Without a strong and healthy ego, we will not be able to grow in awareness and choose the path of true interrelationship with Earth and one another. The ego, however, is given not to be the centre but to serve the centre. It is given not to call attention to itself but to focus on the divine presence at the heart of all being. Our ego needs "the illumination of a holy and whole-making spirit," says Jung.[35] This is the work of the Spirit, or "the uniter of opposites", as he calls it.[36] It is the breath of the divine in our depths that enables us to let go of our ego to serve what is greater than the self, the Life within all life, the Self within all selves.

✻

Because the soul is an "interior microcosm" of the universe, our journey of healing is not something that happens in separation but in relation to all things.[37] It is not a journey that shuts out the world but gathers the world into itself. "Everything hangs together with everything else," said Jung.[38] So, integration in our own depths involves integration with the world. Jung calls it the *unus mundus*, the one world, the interior realm of the soul and the outer realm of the universe conjoined. True wholeness brings the inner and the outer together, the personal and the collective, the soul of the individual and the soul of Earth united.

This shaped Jung's approach to the Christ-figure in his understanding of Christian myth. He saw Christ as manifesting the soul of the world, not simply the soul of a particular individual who lived two thousand years ago. The Christ-figure was archetypal to Jung, revealing "the hidden, unconscious ground-life of every individual".[39] The journey into wholeness, therefore, is not achieved by an imitation of a Christ-figure of the past, as so much religious teaching has given the impression over the centuries. We are not being called to become like another. We are being called to become ourselves and to live from the divine depths of our being. Christ is an icon of the truly human, said Jung, showing us the divinity that is within each of us. As Jesus said to his listeners, "you are gods" (John 10:34). In other words, within you is the divine, waiting to come forth in unique ways from the inner wellspring of your being.

Jung had a powerful dream of Christ on the Cross. He was bathed in bright light and his body was made of "greenish gold".[40] It was a beautiful dream that deeply touched Jung and reminded him of the quest of medieval alchemy, which was to turn so-called "base metals" into "noble metals", and in particular gold. Jung knew, of course, that serious alchemy had never actually been about changing the substance of matter itself. Rather it was about seeking the golden world of the Spirit within this world or, more specifically, accessing the transformative spiritual energies that are deep in the human soul and the body of Earth.

The green gold of Christ's body in the dream spoke to Jung of the relationship between the *anima Christi* (the soul of Christ) and the *anima mundi* (the soul of the world). In essence they are one. Just as Earth's greening power rises from deep within, so the golden essence of the Spirit rises from within us. And the purest gold of our being, Jung believed, is our capacity for love. This for him was the meaning of the dream. Love "bears all things" and "endures all things", as scripture says. "Love never ends" (1 Cor. 13:7–8). These words express it all, said Jung. "Nothing can be added to them."[41] Love is our greatest strength. It rises from the God-essence, or the gold-essence, of our being just as the greening energies of Earth rise from deep within.

If we are to grow in awareness of the oneness of the Christ-mystery and the Cosmos-mystery, and if we are to know in new ways that the inner world of the soul and the outer world of the universe are essentially one, then religious vision needs to be reimagined and expanded. "Christianity slumbers," said Jung, for it has neglected to keep nurturing its essential insights into Earth and the human mystery over the centuries.[42] We need to take its thought-forms that have become historically fixed, he said, and "melt them down again" that we may pour them into new moulds of awareness for this moment in time.[43] In other words, we need to allow our experiences of divine light within us and in all things to reshape our unfolding story of faith for today. We need "to dream the myth onwards," he says, and give it deeper and broader expression.[44] For life "is a flux, a flowing into the future, not a stoppage or backwash."[45] It is not a matter of going back to something that was, trying to make Christianity great again, for instance. It is a matter of allowing our faith to live in ever-new ways, forever flowing into greater and greater awareness.

Jung died on June 6, 1961. Inscribed on his gravestone are words in Latin that he had also etched into stone over the front door of his house in Switzerland, "*Vocatus atque non vocatus, Deus aderit*" (Bidden or not bidden, God is present). Jung had become more and more aware of the presence of the divine in all things. In his BBC *Face to Face* interview with John Freeman just two years before his death, he was asked by Freeman if he believed in God. "I don't need to believe," said Jung. "I know." He had experienced hidden worlds in the world of the soul, and at the heart of it all was God.

If humanity's worst sin is lack of awareness, as Jung had said, then our greatest blessing is to be aware, particularly of the presence of the divine within us and within all things. But for Jung, to be aware, or to know, as he put it, was not the same thing as claiming to understand. He spoke of God as the mystery of love that is beyond understanding, and increasingly he spoke of himself in similar terms. "The older I have become," as he said in his autobiography, "the less I have understood … myself."[46]

Jung resisted fixed systems of thought, including even systems of thought that others had created to systematize his own psychological insights. "I'm glad to be Carl Jung," as he is sometimes quoted as saying, "and not a Jungian." It wasn't fixed systems of thought that he pursued in his life. It was experiential knowledge. And his mind had been humbled by his encounter with the constellations of light that appear beyond numbering in the human soul, galaxy upon galaxy of inner light. In that place of light in our depths he experienced "kinship," as he put it, with everything that has being.[47] Perhaps this is his greatest gift of awareness, knowing the family likeness of all things, the seen and the unseen, the East and the West, the past and the present, the one and the many, humanity and Earth. It is this awareness that led him into a knowing of the deepest mystery, love, the love that calls us to see the other as our self. It is this knowing that will most powerfully serve us in our journey toward wholeness, both individually and together. The journey of awareness is, at the end of the day, a journey of love, love for Earth and one another, and love for ourselves.

MEDITATIVE PRACTICE: SEEKING AWARENESS

Carl Jung is a messenger of awareness to us. He invites us to be alert with love to the light and the shadow, the good and the evil, the beginnings and endings of life that are within us, and to remember the Valley of Diamonds through which we have all travelled in our journey of birth into this world. We come from light, and it is our longing for light that will save us.

> *(pause to listen for what Jung's wisdom stirs in us)*
>
> As morning mist scatters from among the hills
> so my soul longs to see again
> both light and dark
> both height and depth
> the one and the many
> my life and every life
> intertwined
> and each a unique manifestation of the divine.
>
> *(pause to be aware)*
>
> As morning mist scatters from among the hills
> so my soul longs to see again.

Five

Seeking Wellness: Julian of Norwich

All shall be well, and all shall be well, and all manner of things shall be well."[1] These words of benediction come down to us from the fourteenth century. They were written by the English mystic Julian of Norwich (c. 1342–after 1416), who lived through the worst pandemic in recorded history, a time of unimaginable suffering for untold numbers of people throughout the world.

What did Julian mean by "All shall be well"? And what do her words of promise say to us today in our search for well-being, both individually and collectively? How are we and Earth to be well again? The Plague, or the Black Death, as it was later called, arrived in Europe in 1348. Within two years, half the population of England had died. The disease was so fatal, and spread so rapidly, that mass graves were required to deal with the sheer number of deaths, sometimes hundreds and even thousands of bodies buried together five deep in the ground. And that was only the beginning of the pandemic. It kept returning, decade after decade, throughout Julian's lifetime, a devastation that must have seemed endless.

Julian was six years old during the first wave of the pandemic. In her hometown of Norwich, more than half the population died. The young Julian survived the Plague of 1348, but at the age of thirty, during one of the successive waves of the pandemic, she too came close to death. On May 8, 1373, in the middle of the night, a priest was sent for to perform the last rites. And her mother, thinking she had already stopped breathing, reached out her hand to close Julian's eyes. It was at that point, so close to death, that Julian began to receive a dreamlike series of visions, or showings, as she later called them, that came in rapid succession over the next eight hours. They were filled with images of suffering as well as intimations of promise. A final showing came on May 9, like a confirmation of the previous night's experience. And the assurance that came to her throughout was that all shall be well.

Julian did become well again, and almost immediately began to write an account of her visions that we know today as Dame Julian's *Revelations of Divine Love*. In the end she wrote two versions. The first, called the Short Text, was written soon after her recovery from illness. And the second, known as the Long Text, was composed about two decades later, incorporating years of further reflection on her visionary experiences of 1373. To begin with, she assumed that the words *All shall be well* had been meant particularly for her, a promise that she would recover from the disease and be well again. But she soon came to see that the message was universal. It was "addressed to all," she wrote, "because we are all one."[2] What is it that will make us well again?

Julian was a mystic, not a systematic theologian. So, it is best to read her *Revelations of Divine Love* not as a theological treatise, ordered systematically, but rather as a revelatory dream with images rising spontaneously from the unconscious. Its main themes are cyclical. They keep coming again and again in recurring dreamlike patterns. No matter where one dives into her account, the same convergence of themes appears. They are woven together inseparably but the dominant strands are distinct and can be explored one at a time.

First then, deep in Julian's vision of wellness is her awareness that God is the essence of all things. "I saw that God is in everything," she says, and not only *in* everything but the very "*centre* of everything".[3] This for Julian is our ground of well-being. Health is to be found by seeking the source of life deep within us and deep within the body of Earth. God, she says, is "nature's substance".[4] So, let us primarily have faith in nature, not doubt.

This was Julian striking a very different note from the religious teachings that prevailed in fourteenth-century Europe during the Plague. There was widespread fear of the natural world with its capacity for disease and infection. And Church authorities were teaching the people that the pandemic had occurred because of humanity's sinfulness. A vengeful God was using nature to punish humanity. Julian, on the other hand, hears God saying to her in one of her visions, "It is I who am highest; it is I who am lowest; it is I who am all."[5]

God is the essence of all life. We are not simply made *by* God, says Julian, we are "made *of* God".[6] Deep within us and the body of Earth, therefore, is the wisdom of the divine, deeper than the ignorance of what we have done. Deep within us is the creativity of God, deeper than any barrenness in our lives or world. And deep within us and the natural world are the healing energies of the divine and the ability to come back into true relationship with the source of well-being deep in all things. How do we access these depths of healing within ourselves and within the natural world?

"I saw no difference between God and our essential being," says Julian.[7] And our essential being, or our spirit, she says, is bound inextricably to our "sensory being", that is our body.[8] The spiritual and the physical are so interwoven within us that together "they may rightly be called our soul," says Julian.[9] And in our soul, that is, in our body and spirit, we can find everything, for in our soul we can find God.

In one of her visions, she sees that the soul is like "an endless world".[10] And to know our soul is to know God. "We can never attain full knowledge of God," she says, "until we first know our own soul clearly."[11] The relationship between our inner being and the essence of the divine is like a knotwork of everlasting design in which one strand is woven inseparably around the other so that it is impossible to see where the one begins and the other ends. It is an interweaving "so subtle and so strong," says Julian, that we are forever joined to God and God is forever joined to us.[12] Prayer, then, is about reuniting with the divine at the heart of our being and, thus, reconnecting to our true depths and the true depths of everything that has being.

To speak of the oneness of God with our true depths and with Earth is not to neglect the reality of disease and suffering. Our lives, says Julian, are a mixture of "weal and woe".[13] We know blessing and goodness in life as well as pain and sorrow. We know loss and grieving, and we also know birth and new beginnings.

The pandemic of the fourteenth century brought terrible devastation across the globe. Julian witnessed it all around her and experienced something of it personally in her own close encounter with death. The stench of disease and decay was everywhere, especially in crowded cities like Norwich. Images of death and dying, therefore, appear in her visions. Julian invites us to look directly at suffering rather than to deny it or downplay it. "I saw a body lying on the earth," she says, "a body which looked dismal and ugly, without shape or form as if it were a swollen and heaving mass of stinking mire."[14]

In Julian's visions, she sees Christ as an expression of humanity in both its sufferings and its glory. As she lay in her sickbed, close to death, she saw "the body of Christ bleeding abundantly, hot and freshly and vividly The blood ran so abundantly," she said, "that if at that moment it had been natural blood, the whole bed would have been blood-soaked and even the floor around."[15]

The path to wellness does not take us around pain and struggle in our lives and world. Rather, it leads us into a deeper awareness of life's sorrows as well as life's joys. In one of her visions, Julian sees in Christ's countenance a profound knowing of sorrow. Indeed, the beauty of his face, as she describes it, is characterized by an awareness of both the glory and the anguish of life. "His eyes were black," she says, "most comely and handsome, appearing full of tender pity." And the "handsome mixture" in his face was "partly sorrow and pity, partly joy and bliss."[16] This is the beauty of soul that we are being invited to know and live, a compassionate awareness of the woe as well as the weal of life, the gift of Earth's magnificence and the pain of Earth's labour, the laughter of family and friends and the tears of loss and grief. And we can choose to live this beauty of soul for the sake of one another's wellness and for the sake of Earth's wellness. For, as we shall see, to Julian they are one. Our well-being and the well-being of all things belong inseparably together.

Awareness is for Julian integral to the way of wellness, whether that be awareness of God as the essence of life or awareness of the ways we have failed to honour the sacred in one another and nature. Julian wants us to name our failings, and to consciously confront them, without allowing them to dominate our perspective, as has been the case in so much religious teaching and practice in the Western world, to the extent that sin has often been described by church doctrine as our essence, opposed to God instead of grounded in God. Although Julian wants us to name and confront sin, she also wants to say that it has "no sort of substance" in and by itself, even though it is the cause of physical and spiritual suffering.[17] "You are nothing," she says to sin in one of her reflections, for you are not rooted in the true essence of life. "When I saw that God had made all things, I saw nothing of you," says Julian. "And when I saw that God is in all things, I saw nothing of you ... And so I am certain that you are nothing."[18] And when we choose to follow sin, she continues, we are choosing nothing. In the end sin burns itself out with falseness and destructiveness. It is contrary to God and the sacredness of nature and, thus, has no ultimate future. It is "unnatural", she says, and leads in the end to nonexistence.[19]

Although Julian sees that sin has no eternal substance, she also sees clearly that it causes agony. We, therefore, "really do need to see it," she says.[20] We need to name it for what it is and denounce it within ourselves and within the world as the source of suffering and evil. But we are not to give it greater status than what it has. Being conscious of it, however, is essential. For if we do not recognize it within us, and within our communities and nations, we will not be truly well for we will lack "humility", she says.[21] We will have forgotten that our essential well-being resides not in anything of our own achieving or attaining but in the ground or *humus* of our being and that we will be well in our depths only to the extent that we remain firmly rooted in the divine deep in all things. Everything else is passing.

We need to turn from our failings and denounce wrongdoing whenever it appears among us, but it is important not to focus on the sins of others, says Julian, unless we can do so with compassion and "a holy wish for God to help them".[22] Preoccupation with other people's sins, as deplorable and colourful as they may be, "makes a sort of thick mist before the eyes of the soul," she says.[23] And we no longer clearly see our own need for healing and our own need for grace.

God shows us our weaknesses, says Julian, but only in the light of divine mercy so that we may return to our true nature. Grace is given not to make us something other than ourselves but to make us truly ourselves. It is given not that we might become more than natural or other than natural but that we might become truly natural. It is given, says Julian, to "bring fair kind nature back to the blessed point from which it came, that is God."[24] Grace is like the dispensing of "medicine" by the Spirit to allow the true source of our well-being to flow again from deep within us and free us from the unnaturalness of what we have become.[25] "Nature and grace are in harmony," says Julian, "for grace is God as nature is God."[26]

What if Western Christianity had clearly seen the oneness of nature and grace? It would have allowed our religion to ground itself in the natural world, and honour it, rather than lift itself above the natural world, and exploit it. It would have freed us to experience grace as completing our nature instead of suppressing our nature. And, after failure in our lives, says Julian, we would have been able to see "the scars of

[our] healed wounds" not as disfiguring our essence but as ennobling the countenance of our soul, like a mighty tree that has weathered the brunt of storm and bears within itself the marks of struggle and loss.[27] Not a perfect tree, and not necessarily a pretty sight, but a tree of unique character and history manifesting the nobility of its nature and its God-given capacity for new life.

*

It seems that Julian was a laywoman at the time of her illness and visionary experiences of 1373. And some scholars suggest that she also may have been a widow and a bereaved mother at the time, given the widespread impact of disease on families and especially young children during the successive waves of the pandemic. By 1393, however, when she was writing the longer account of her visions, she was a religious solitary living in a cell attached to St. Julian's Church in Norwich. So, it may be that "Julian" was not her birth name but rather the name she adopted upon becoming a religious recluse attached to the church so named.

One of the main themes to emerge repeatedly in Julian's dreamlike series of visions is the interrelatedness of all things and all people. In God's sight, she says, we are all "one" or, as she puts it elsewhere, we are "one soul".[28] Part of what this means is that the revelations given to her, as she sees early on, belong not simply to her but to the whole of humanity. And the journey into wellness that she seeks in her life is the wellness that is intended for all people and for all life.

It is significant that Julian chose to live in a cell attached to a church on a busy street in Norwich rather than choosing a cloistered life in a rural monastic community. Her cell had two windows. One opened onto the hustle and bustle of Norwich, a city of international trade and commerce. Through this window she heard the news and gossip of her local community, and through this window she would also listen to the struggles and hopes of individuals who came to her for spiritual guidance and counsel. The other window in her cell opened into the main sanctuary of the church. Through this window she heard the prayers and chanting of daily services in the church and received the sacrament of communion. Julian was living in a place of interconnection between the blessings and work of daily life, on the one hand, and the grace and ministrations of religion on the other. She is an expression of the meeting place between spiritual discipline and daily life, and of the relationship between the mystical and the so-called ordinary.

In one of her visions, she sees in the palm of her hand "a little thing, the size of a hazel nut … round as any ball." When she asks what this can be, she hears the Spirit saying, "It is all that is made." And in this little thing she sees three attributes. "The first is that God made it, the second is that God loves it, [and] the third is that God cares for it."[29] A microcosm of the macrocosm, everything as one, round as a ball. "The fullness of joy," Julian says, "is to see God in everything."[30] Not just in one thing or one person, not just in one nation or one species but in everything that has being. And she comes to understand wholeness as the curve of inter-relationship between all things, not in separation but together.

There is somebody in Julian's life, "a certain person whom I loved," she says. And she asks God how it will be for that person. We don't know who that person is. Is it a man, a woman, a child? We don't know. And is that individual sick or struggling or in pain? Again, we don't know. What we do know is that Julian particularly loves this person and longs for their well-being. But the answer that she receives to her question is that it is more important to consider God "in all things than in any particular thing", and to seek wellness not simply for those we particularly love but to seek wellness for all.[31] The promise she hears in her soul is that "all shall be well, and all shall be well, and all manner of things shall be well."

Who are these special ones in our lives? The people we particularly love and cherish, our sons and daughters, our brothers and sisters, our parents, our beloved, our friends. Or the places that are dear to us and the creatures who have blessed us with their beauty and faithfulness.

Or the nations we are proud of, the ancestral home of our peoples and families. Like Julian, we too ask how it will be for these ones. We of course long for their well-being.

*

When my eldest son, Brendan, was sixteen, he suffered a major psychotic breakdown. Suddenly he was cast into a world of fear and anxiety that toppled at times into full-blown paranoia. And suddenly all the hopes and expectations we as a family had for him were dashed. Would he ever be well again? And would he be able to live the life we had always hoped for him? It was a staggering time of uncertainty and doubt in our lives as a family. And our deepest prayer of longing for him was that he should be well.

A major turning point came for us when we realized as a family that Brendan's illness was not simply his. It was ours. And it was ours not only as a family but ours as a society and world. Through Brendan we came to know other young men and women struggling with mental illness. And what we learned through them, and through our Brendan, was that these beautiful and often artistic young men and women are highly perceptive and sensitive spirits, and that our world, driven as it is by fear and hostility, is too much for them. It breaks them. Thus, we came to see more clearly that their struggle is not simply theirs. It belongs to us all. They are manifesting the symptoms of an unwellness that is ours as a world and as nations.

It made me realize in a new way that healing comes not in isolation but together. And that we will not be truly well as a society until these young ones are well, and that they will not be truly well until we as a world are well. Not that we are to passively wait until our society and world are well before passionately giving ourselves to the healing of these cherished ones in our lives. But the wellness that we long for individually, and in our family life, will come only to the extent that we seek healing also for the whole. They belong inseparably together. The healing that has come in Brendan's life, as is the case with the healing that comes for any part of the whole, whether that be the healing of life-forms that are struggling because of what humanity is doing to the environment, or races that are suffering because of the widespread sickness of racism in our world, or families that are enduring the cruelty of poverty because of the prevailing inequities of society, these are healed not in isolation but in interrelationship. And in Brendan's case, the extent of wellness that he now knows in his life has come not in isolation but through family, through networks of mental health support and medical provision, through friends, through a loving partner, through nature, and not least of all through the unflagging energies of a border collie that gets him out into the hills of the Scottish Highlands every day! And, of course, his wellness comes also from the fount of healing that is deep in his own soul, made of God.

All shall be well, and all shall be well, and all manner of things shall be well.

During the fourteenth-century pandemic, there was a tragic forgetting of the interrelationship of the parts to the whole. There were segments of society that chose to look after themselves alone, at the expense of others. The poor were especially prone to infection, living in crowded and often unhygienic conditions in the cities. The rich and powerful, on the other hand, were often able to escape the cities to the relative safety of their country estates. This bred ill will and antagonism among the poor toward those in authority and privilege, a growing discontent that spilled over into violence later in the century, as was the case in England during the Peasants' Revolt of 1381.

But even more tragic than social discontent, and the violence it gave rise to, was the tendency during the Plague to scapegoat minority groups in society and to blame them for the pandemic. The worst hit were Jewish communities throughout Europe. They were accused of poisoning the waters or intentionally spreading disease. In September 1348 the municipality of Zurich voted never to admit Jews to the city again. And, in Basel, Jewish families were penned up in wooden buildings and burned alive. Over the next few years tens of thousands of Jews were massacred and many Jewish communities disappeared altogether from large swaths of Europe.

Close to the heart of Julian's vision of promise is that wellness belongs to the whole, not to special individuals or segments of society. It is this that God delights in, she says, our oneness. So, well-being can never be the preserve of one people over another, nor can it be achieved by one race, one nation, one gender, or one species at the expense of the rest. The promise is not that one shall be well but that all shall be well.

A significant aspect of Julian's vision of wellness is the balance between the feminine and the masculine that she celebrates, an integration that was tragically absent in fourteenth-century religion and society. The place of women was in the hiddenness of domestic life, of birthing and caring and serving in the family home, not in the public domain of creativity and leadership and governance. In 1349 in an account from the Bishop of Bath and Wells, the bishop expresses concern about many of his parishes being without priests, either through the high rate of death among clergy during the pandemic or through an unwillingness of the remaining clergy to visit the sick for fear of infection. In particular, he is concerned that many people are dying without access to the Sacrament of Penance to confess their sins before death. "If they are on the point of death and cannot secure the services of a priest, then they should make confession to each other," writes the bishop, "or, if no man is present, even to a woman."[32]

Even to a woman! This sums up the place of the feminine in fourteenth-century England. In radical distinction to this, Julian celebrates the sacred dignity of womanhood. "God is our mother as truly as God is our father," she says.[33] We and all things have come from the womb of the divine. She speaks in her writings of the motherhood of nature, the motherhood of grace, and the motherhood of love. To be made of "kind nature", as Julian says, and to be completed by grace, is to know that we have been born from the womb of the divine and loved into fullness through the feminine graces of God.

There is no public mention of the writings of Julian during her lifetime. It seems that she kept them safe in her Norwich cell. There would have been no place of outward recognition for the writings of a woman in fourteenth-century England, especially writings that were so at odds with the teaching authorities of the church. Her visions were in stark contrast to the doctrine of original sin that prevailed in Western theology and the belief in a judgmental Father-God who punished humanity for its sinfulness. Julian saw us not as essentially sinful but as essentially divine. And her visions focused on the boundless mercy and love of the divine.

She was the first writer in English whom we can identify with certainty as a woman. But it was not until three hundred years after her visionary experiences that her writings first appeared in print. That was two hundred years after the development of the printing press in England and the early publications of her contemporary Geoffrey Chaucer. And, even then, the earliest publication of her work was available only to a few. Her *Revelations* did not emerge from obscurity until 1901 when a manuscript of the Long Text was found in the British Museum Library and transcribed and published with notes by the Scottish editor and translator Grace Warrack. Significantly the manuscript appeared, as is often the case with neglected wisdom, when it was desperately needed, in the dangerously male-dominated modern world of the twentieth century, an age characterized by war on a scale never known before and a threat to Earth's well-being that is now imperilling the very future of humanity.

✽

About fifteen years after her illness and the initial account of her showings, Julian received a final revelation. She had often longed to know what the essential meaning of her series of visions in 1373 was. Finally, fifteen years later, she received an answer. "Love was what God meant," she hears. "Who showed you this? Love. What did God show? Love. Why did God show it to you? For love."[34] Thus it is that Julian's visions eventually became known to the world as the *Revelations of Divine Love*. Love is their essence. We are "made for love", as she says.[35] And it is through love that we will be remade.

"On the last day," says Julian, God will do a "deed" that will make all things well. She doesn't claim to know exactly what that deed is or when it will occur or how it will come about. It remains "unknown to all creatures," she says.[36] But when Julian speaks of "the last day", it is unlikely that she is primarily making a chronological point. More important, she is making an essential point or an eternal point, a point that relates to the beginning and the end, to the making of life and its remaking. And her words invite us to be looking for that divine deed with expectation and hope, and to be asking how we can be part of it now for one another and for the healing of Earth.

Julian sees that "the soul is highest, noblest and worthiest when it is lowest, humblest and gentlest."[37] What is the deed that is highest and lowest, that takes the form not of domination and force but of humility and gentleness, and that does not impose itself on the other but offers itself in grace? "I have always loved you," hears Julian, "and [I] love you now."[38] Love is our beginning and our end. It is love that has given birth to Earth and the human soul, and it is love that will make us well again.

God has loved us into being and longs for our well-being. And this same love is deep in us for we are made of God. Julian calls it the "love-longing" of the divine that knows no end.[39] Deep in our souls we long for the well-being of Earth and one another. We may be tragically cut off from this love-longing, and we may have forgotten what will truly satisfy it, but it is deep within us, waiting to rise again. "The desire of the soul," says Julian, "is the desire of God."[40] Our deepest yearnings, both physical and spiritual, are for love. We long to be united again with the divine at the heart of one another and all things. "It is I you love," she hears, "it is I you long for; it is I you desire; it is I who am your purpose; it is I who am everything."[41] Julian thus sees that we are being invited to "enjoy love in everything", for God is the essence of all things.[42] And when we are fully reawakened to our true depths we will find ourselves "seeing" God, "feeling" God, "hearing" God, "smelling" God, and "tasting" God in all things.[43] It is God's desire, she says, that we should know oneness and live together in "unending love".[44]

Only when we love will we be truly well. This is what "our salvation means," she says.[45] We will be "saved" when we love everything that has being, for only then will we be living from our true depths and honouring the true depths of Earth and one another.[46] Hold fast to this vision, she hears, and "you shall not be overcome".[47] It is love that will make us well.

Julian makes it clear that God did not say to her, "You shall not be tormented, you shall not be troubled, you shall not be grieved." The words of promise are "you shall not be overcome". We will know pain in our lives, and there will be struggle and loss, but love will save us. This is the meaning of Julian's revelations. And this is why we have been born, she says, to love. So, whether we live or die, whether we know sorrow or joy, whether those dearest to us are suffering or in health, whether we are in the beautiful wildness of nature or in the decimated landscape of a city, love. For love is our "beginning", says Julian. And love is our true "end".[48] It is love that will make us well.

Six hundred years after the Black Death and Julian's vision of hope, England was again living through a harrowing and uncertain time, 1942

and the Nazi bombing of London in which thousands were being killed. Hitler had conquered most of Europe and an invasion of England seemed imminent. It was in that year, 1942, with bombs dropping all around him in London, that the English poet T.S. Eliot wrote "Little Gidding", a poem in which he drew inspiration from Julian:

> We shall not cease from exploration
> And the end of all our exploring
> Will be to arrive where we started
> And know the place for the first time.
> …
> And all shall be well and
> All manner of thing shall be well[49]

Eliot did not know how things would turn out for England or himself or for those whom he most loved. But with Julian he knew that in our beginning, made of love, is our end. And if we are faithful to love, we are drawing from a well deep within our souls that will never be exhausted. It is our true fount of well-being, and our source of new beginnings.

Made for love. Made of love. Made to love. This is the essence of Julian's vision. And it is the heart of the promise that she speaks to us in her revelations. "All shall be well, and all shall be well, and all manner of things shall be well."

MEDITATIVE PRACTICE: SEEKING WELLNESS

Julian of Norwich is a messenger of wellness to us. She invites us to seek it now and to know that the wellness of the part and the wellness of the whole belong inseparably together. She calls us to look suffering in the face, to feel it and name it, and to ground our hope for healing in the love-longings of the Spirit deep within us, love for those we cherish, love for Earth, love for all. For it is together that we shall be well.

(pause to listen for what Julian's wisdom stirs in us)

As a wounded creature longs for healing
so my soul longs to be well
and for all to be well
healing for Earth
justice for the creatures
and peace for the human family
that we may live together on Earth the promise of Heaven.

(pause to be aware)

As a wounded creature longs for healing
so my soul longs to be well.

Six

Seeking Love: Jalaluddin Rumi

Jalaluddin Rumi (1207–1273) is one of the most widely read poets in the Western world today. Interestingly, he is also extremely popular in the Islamic Republic of Iran, a nation which, despite its name, is becoming increasingly secular. In both the Middle East and the West, then, Rumi's poetry is being celebrated as part of a spiritual search that is happening in the context of large-scale exile from religion. A Sufi poet of the thirteenth century is speaking directly into the heart of the spiritual quest of this moment in time, and especially into its yearnings for a spirituality of love. Love, says Rumi, is the "true religion".[1] Everything else is like a thrown-away bandage.

In Sufi contemplative practice, the reed flute (called the *ney*) is cherished for its sound of longing. In each note, says Rumi, we hear the instrument yearning for the reedbed from which it has come. And we hear too the sound of the human soul longing for home and the love from which it has come. Listen to the story, says Rumi, told by the *ney* of being separated from its source:

> Since I was cut from the reedbed,
> I have made this crying sound.
> Anyone apart from someone he loves
> understands what I say.
> Anyone pulled from a source
> longs to go back.[2]

A "love fire" burns in the music of the flute, says Rumi.³ It is the sound of intimacy and longing for intimacy. And the song it sings, he says, is also our song, for each one of us carries "a longing-pain" for the One from whom we have come. This One is our Beloved, says Rumi, the source of our life and the fount of love. "Be your note" in the singing of this song, says Rumi. "Sing loud!"⁴ Give expression to the love-longings that are at the heart of your being.

Rumi was born in Afghanistan, part of the Persian Empire at the time. But, at the age of ten, Rumi and his family fled their homeland as war refugees under the threat of Mongol invasion. They settled in Turkey where his father established a madrassa, a school for the study of the Quran, in the town of Konya. After his father's death, Rumi took up headship of the school and until the age of forty appears to have been a traditional Islamic scholar and religious teacher. This all changed in the autumn of 1244 with the arrival of a wandering Sufi mystic, Shams of Tabriz.

We know little about Shams. His name means "Sun", and to Rumi he was like a wild sun-lion shining with a spiritual light that was greater than doctrine and theology. Upon arrival in Konya, Shams lived on the outskirts of town among the homeless and travellers. And in his teachings, he drew not from the study of learned theologians but from direct experience of the divine. Rumi immediately opened his heart to him, and in the mystical conversations that ensued between the two men Rumi came to see that love is the lens through which the mystery of God is to be accessed. "Earth-love, spirit-love, any love," as he later said.⁵ They are all expressions of relationship with the Beloved. The "love inside love", as he put it, the spiritual fire that burns deep in every true expression of love is what he calls "the resurrection place".⁶ It is the place of new beginnings. Whether it be love for another person or love of Earth or love of the great luminaries of the skies – the sun, moon and stars moving forever in harmony – love is the deepest source of new life.

When Shams used the term *Allaha akbar*, which in translation reads "God is greater", he did not mean "my God is greater than your God" or "the God of Islam is greater than the God of Christianity or Judaism", as is so often conveyed when militant Islamists call out the phrase in places of conflict and terror in the world. By *Allaha akbar* Shams meant "God is greater than that which you have imagined."[7] And, so, although Sufis speak of there being ninety-nine names of God, the true name of the divine is the one hundredth name. And that name is unknown. It is beyond our imagining and cannot be expressed. This is the case also with divine love. As Rumi later wrote, "A pen went scribbling along, but when it tried to write *love*, it broke."[8] To try to define it is impossible. Love, in its many forms, needs to be experienced to be known.

After Shams's arrival in Konya and Rumi's "conversion" to love, he began to teach in new ways. No longer was Islamic law and doctrine his main source. His goal now as a teacher was to touch the heart of his listeners, to enable them to become lovers of God. He started to use music and dance and poetry to instruct his people. And he encouraged them to know God directly rather than to just know *about* God through the teachings and experiences of others. Don't be satisfied with the stories of others, he said. "Unfold your own myth."[9] Open yourself to experience the love of the divine directly through one another and all things. And allow this to be the story at the heart of your faith. "Love-religion has no code or doctrine," he said. It has "only God". Those who pay attention primarily to religious ways of behaving and speaking are one sort. "Lovers who burn," said Rumi, "are another."[10]

> So, today when you wake,
> Don't open the door to the study and begin reading.
> Take down a musical instrument.

Seeking Love: Jalaluddin Rumi 115

Let the beauty we love be what we do.
There are hundreds of ways to kneel and kiss the ground.
Out beyond ideas of wrongdoing and right doing,
there is a field. I'll meet you there.
When the soul lies down in that grass,
the world is too full to talk about.
Ideas, language, even the phrase *each other*
doesn't make any sense.
The breeze at dawn has secrets to tell you.
Don't go back to sleep.
You must ask for what you really want.
Don't go back to sleep.
People are going back and forth across the door-sill
where the two worlds touch.
The door is round and open.
Don't go back to sleep.[11]

"I belong to the beloved," said Rumi, and I "have seen the two worlds as one."[12] It is love that enables us to know that heaven and Earth belong inseparably together, that spirit and matter are forever conjoined, and that the divine and the human kiss in the intimate depths of our souls. Rumi calls us to rid religion of everything about it that is not inspired by love. The challenge is as simple as that. And equally demanding.

Years ago, I was frequently able to join a Sufi community in New Mexico for their weekly celebration of *zikr*. It is a ritual of remembering that everything is God. The phrase that is repeated, both inwardly in silence and outwardly in speech during the ritual, is *La ilaha ill Allah* ("There is no reality but God, there is only God"). Kneeling together on the carpeted floor of a yurt in northern New Mexico, with our shoulders touching, we chanted the names of God as we rocked forward and backward, again and again, moving as one in an ecstasy of prayer.

One of the first times I experienced *zikr* I was kneeling next to the leader of the Sufi community, men on one side of the yurt and women opposite, also swaying in motion together. I could feel his body next to mine moving with such ease and rhythm, forward and backward, his hands and forehead touching the floor with each repetition of one of the holy names. On the other side of me, also shoulder to shoulder, was Cameron, my youngest son, about ten years of age at the time. To begin with I could feel his young body unsure about the ecstatic movement, and I could hear his voice hesitating in the repetition of divine names. But after a while he began to rock, forward and backward, moving freely, again and again, and I could hear his voice growing in confidence, his soul like a reed calling out for home.

I will always cherish that moment. Together we were offering ourselves in prayer, our breath, our bodies, our voices, our souls. The spirituality writer Barbara Brown Taylor speaks of "holy envy".[13] It is a beautiful way of saying that sometimes another tradition offers us an experience of the divine that we don't typically experience in our own. This doesn't mean that we set out to imitate the other tradition. But there are things that we can reverently learn from all traditions. And for me in that moment I realized I wanted to learn to let go, both physically and spiritually, in devotion to love. It was a yearning not only for myself but for my son and the people of my tradition, that we may find ways of experiencing love together in worship, in our bodies as well as our souls. This is part of the Great Search of today, to find ways of prayer and meditative awareness that can be part of our healing and take us closer to home again in relation to Earth and our spiritual depths.

*

Five times a day in Islam there is a call to prayer, *salat*, as it is called – prayer at dawn and noon, in the midafternoon and sunset, and finally again at nightfall. If one is in a predominantly Muslim country or close enough to a minaret to hear the enchanting sound of the muezzin calling the people to prayer, one hears the words *La ilaha ill Allah* ("There is no reality but God, there is only God"). It is a reminder that although our outward physical existence has a type of reality to it, it is a passing reality. "This here-and-now mountain," as Rumi says, "is a tiny piece of a piece of straw."[14] There will come a day when it is no more. But this is not to disparage the outward and the physical. For love delights in the body – in the body of Earth and in the human body. The physical world is like an icon through which we are invited to see the beauty of the eternal world shining within us and among us. "The body," says Rumi, "lets you glimpse the glitter on the water of the soul."[15]

Our physicalness is in fact so cherished in Islam that there is a prayer for different parts of the human body. This, of course, for Rumi leads not only to reverence but to humour. He tells the story of a man who ended up saying the wrong prayer for the wrong part of the body. Reciting the nose prayer, which is all about seeking to breathe in the fragrance of the divine, the man placed his hands by mistake not on his nose but on his bottom!

The physical, in both its beauty and absurdity, is passing. The only ultimate reality is God. But we are not to look for the divine presence as if it were entirely beyond us or above us. "The moon," says Rumi. "The full moon is inside your house."[16] So don't be thinking that you will find it only up in the sky. "Learn that your own essence is your wealth," he says.[17] The waters of life that your soul longs for are deep within you. So draw from the inner well of your being instead of thinking that you can only "drink from other people's waterbags".[18] Be courageous and discipline yourself, says Rumi. "Keep digging your well."[19] The water is there. And it will flow from your depths when you open to the river of the divine that is deep within you.

There is a "spring-source" that rises under everything, says Rumi.[20] It has been flowing in all things since the beginning of time. And always we have been part of Earth's unfolding journey:

> We began
> as a mineral. We emerged into plant life
> and into the animal state, and then into being human,
> and always we have forgotten our former states,
> except in early spring when we slightly recall
> being green again …
> Humankind is being led along an evolving course
> … and though we seem to be sleeping,
> there is an inner wakefulness
> that directs the dream,
> and will eventually startle us back
> to the truth of who we are.[21]

It is this "inner wakefulness" of soul that Rumi is inviting us to be part of, and to be alert to the spring-source of the divine that flows in all things. Everything is evolving, and the physical world is passing like a dream, but within it all is the shining presence of the Beloved inviting us into relationship. So, "make peace with the universe," says Rumi. "Take joy in it. It will turn to gold. Resurrection will be now. Every moment, a new beauty." The promise of new life is not about the future. It is about the present. "Taste the *here* and the *now* of God," says Rumi. There is no need to look for a coming age of bliss. It is now. Our deepest needs and our deepest desires can be met in the gift of this moment. Here and now, says Rumi, "cash in hand".[22]

It is something of this joy, even ecstasy, that communicates itself in the form of spiritual dance attributed to Rumi. Legend has it that he was walking in the gold-smithing section of Konya when he heard in the rhythmic hammering of the artisans the sound of music. He began turning in harmony with the sound, ecstatically surrendering himself to the moment. "We have fallen into the place where everything is music," he says.[23] And Rumi comes to know this harmony deep in all things, in the music of the heavenly spheres and what he calls the "secret turning" of the universe. So, turn as the Earth and moon turn, he says, "circling what they love."[24]

The word universe is derived from the Latin *uni* meaning "one" and *verse* meaning "turn". The universe consists of one great turning. Everything is moving in relation to everything else. We now know that the Earth is revolving around the sun at a speed of sixty-seven thousand miles an hour, and that our whole solar system is whirling around the centre of the Milky Way at a speed of five hundred thousand miles an hour. We are part of one great cosmic dance, spinning our way through the infinity of space at nearly six hundred thousand miles per hour. Even the tiny dust particles that we see whirling in daylight, says Rumi, are part of the one great turning of all things.

The whirling dervishes, as they came to be known in the Sufi tradition, reflect this turning. They are seen as placing themselves at the doorway where the two worlds touch, and then spinning in ecstasy. Their right hand is held high above them, palm upwards to receive blessings from the eternal world, and their left hand is reaching out, palm downwards, to channel blessings to the people and creatures of Earth. And, as they spin, they are aware of the promise from the Quran, "Whichever way you turn, there is the face of God" (The Cow 2.115). Their countenances shine as they circle the One they love in all things.

It is important to remember that Rumi stands firmly within a particular religious tradition. He is not a New Age mystic. He is a faithful son of Islam. "Flee to God's Quran," he says, "take refuge in it."[25] Merge there with the spirit of the prophets. And yet his faithfulness to the spirit of Islam leads him not to ignore the wisdom of other great religious traditions but to honour their insights and learn from their vision. "I go into the Muslim mosque and the Jewish synagogue and the Christian church," says Rumi, "and I see one altar."[26] He sees a single devotion of heart amid a multiplicity of form and expression. "All these religions, all this singing," he says, but "One Song":

> The differences are just illusion and vanity.
> Sunlight looks different on this wall
> than it does on that wall,
> and a whole lot different
> on this wall over here,
> but it is still sunlight.
> … Just as one man can be a father to you
> brother to another and uncle to yet another,
> what you are searching for has many names
> but one existence.
> Stop looking for [just] one of the names.
> Move beyond attachment to names.
> Every war and conflict between human beings
> has happened because of some disagreement about the names.
> It's such unnecessary foolishness
> because just beyond the arguing,
> where we are all one people,
> there is a long table of companionship
> beautifully set
> and just waiting for us to sit down [together].[27]

Rumi can be seen as the Muslim equivalent of John the Beloved in Christian tradition who said, "God is love, and those who abide in love abide in God, and God abides in them" (1 John 4:16). Like Rumi, John is a prophet of love as the true religion. And they both see Jesus as a messenger of this love. Rumi says of him that through love Jesus "opens a door to the other world."[28] He leads us into the eternal world at the heart of this world. And, in his reverence for Jesus, Rumi is not an exception to Islam. Rather, he is a poetic expression of what his own tradition holds dear.

※

Years ago, when I used to visit the high desert of New Mexico every summer to teach at Ghost Ranch Education and Retreat Center north of Santa Fe, I would always do some work with a wise woman from the nearby Sufi community of Abiquiu. Her name is Rahmah, based on a word that is used many times in the Quran to speak of the mercy and compassion of God. In Arabic the literal meaning of the word is "womb". So, her name is used to remember the merciful and compassionate essence of the divine and the maternal womb of love from which we and all things have come.

One morning, when it was my turn to teach, I invited our retreatants to meditate on the words of John the Beloved from Christian scripture, "God is love, and those who abide in love abide in God, and God abides in them." Some chose to reflect outside, walking meditatively in the desert landscape, silently repeating the words within themselves. Others remained inside in silence, sitting in the adobe chapel with its doors wide open to the new day's light. It was then that I noticed Rahmah's countenance. She was sitting opposite me in the circle, and her face was shining like the radiance of a full moon.

When the group gathered again to share their reflections with one another, Rahmah was the first to speak. She said, "I so love Jesus. Peace be upon him. He is so merciful and compassionate. I so love Jesus. Peace be upon him." Most of us sitting in the circle that day were Christians. We sat gazing at Rahmah, many of us with tears in our eyes, thinking, *Rahmah, you are teaching us how to speak about Jesus.*

Sometimes it is someone from another tradition who will help point us again to the heart of our own tradition. "Peace be upon him" is the phrase of reverence used in Islam every time the Prophet Mohammed's name is spoken. And every chapter, or *sura*, of the Quran begins with the words, "In the name of God, the Compassionate and the Merciful." Rahmah was using the most cherished words of her tradition to speak of Jesus. What if we too were to learn to speak of Jesus, not with the Church's language of doctrine and creed, but with the vocabulary of love uttered from the heart? "I so love Jesus. Peace be upon him. He is so merciful and compassionate." And what if we were to learn also to speak of the great prophetic figures of other traditions with such reverence?

Like Rahmah, Rumi too loves Jesus. When he describes God as the brilliance of pure light that is refracted into the many colours of creation, he speaks of the whiteness of light that shines in Jesus, a combination of all the colours, a pure emanation of the divine. Rumi is inviting us to learn to speak poetically and imaginatively of Jesus, pointing to the light we love in him rather than attempting to pin down the mystery of his being with the fixed terminology of religious dogma.

"Jesus was lost in love for God," says Rumi, and "his donkey was drunk with barley."[29] He can be wonderfully playful in his approach to Jesus:

> I called through [the door of my neighbour] …
> "The mystics are gathering
>   in the street" [I said]. "Come out!"
> "Leave me alone" [said my neighbour]
> "I'm sick."
> "I don't care if you're dead!" [I replied]
> "Jesus is here, and he wants
>   to resurrect somebody!"[30]

For Rumi, Jesus is a manifestation of the resurrection-force that is deep in all things. "Spring is Christ," he says, "raising martyred plants from their shrouds."[31] Within every human being and every life-form is the

Seeking Love: Jalaluddin Rumi 123

intermingling of the two worlds – Heaven and Earth, the seen and the unseen, spirit and matter. So, for Rumi, we are all bearers of the Christ mystery:

> The body is like Mary and each of us has a Christ inside.
> Who is not in labour, holy labour? Every creature is …
> Yes, God also needs to be born,
> birth from a hand's loving touch,
> birth from a song breathing life into the world.
> The body is like Mary, and each of us, each of us,
> has a Christ within.[32]

The divine-human intermingling in our depths, the "resurrection place" of love, as Rumi calls it, expresses itself most truly in our lives through humility. It is the path of *humus*, living close to the ground, rather than the way of *hubris*, lifting ourselves up over others. As the Quran says, "Do not walk proudly on Earth. You cannot rival the mountains in stature" (Al-Isra 17.37). And never say or think that you are better than others, says Rumi. "That's what Satan thought."[33]

Rumi is referring here to the story of God bringing forth Adam from the moist soil of Earth and breathing life into him. The Quran describes God instructing the angels to bow to this expression of the two worlds intermingling, spirit and matter, the soil of Earth and the breath of Heaven forming humanity. The story recounts how the whole host of heaven then bows in reverence, with one exception. Satan, the greatest angel of light, refuses, saying he will not bow to what God has brought forth from the "black moulded loam" of Earth (Al-Hijr 15.33). This, says Rumi, is the beginning of Satan's falseness. And it is also our path of falseness when we arrogantly lift ourselves up over one another and over Earth.

The word *Islam* means "surrender". It also means "peace". To surrender to the will of the divine at the heart of our being is the foundation of true peace in our lives and world. To surrender to the divine this way is not to demean ourselves or lessen the dignity of our being. Rather, it is the way to free ourselves from the tyranny of the ego and live from our true essence, made of God. Rumi speaks of the "great *jihad*". This is not about waging war on others, whether that be other nations or other religions. It is about waging war on the false self and living from our true depths. There is no room in the inner chamber of our being for the "big ego-beast" and all its baggage, he says.[34] It needs to go. And this is as true of us collectively as it is individually. The great ego-beast of our nation or religion or species needs to go that we may live from our true depths and honour the divine in Earth and one another.

Rumi was known in Konya for stopping to bow to children and old women on the street, to bless and be blessed by them. And he chose to be in relationship with society's outcasts rather than ever seeing himself as greater than them. When "the grape skin of ego breaks," he says, a great pouring begins.[35] The true juice of our being flows, and we are set free to live in love. So, "take an axe to the prison wall" of your ego, says Rumi, and break through.[36] You will find that you have been living in a poor little shack, confined by self, when in fact the foundations of your being are gold. Choose to live in the spacious palace of love – love of Earth, love of one another, and love of your true self.

Surrendering to God is for Rumi about surrendering to love. He calls it "love-madness", when we give ourselves to love without restraint.[37] "Whoever's calm and sensible," he says, is in fact "insane!"[38] For then we miss the heart of life. Although wine is forbidden in Islam, Rumi uses it as a symbol of mystical intoxication, loving God with abandon, and forever seeking to merge with the divine in one another and all things. There is a "love-lion" grazing in the pasture of your soul, says Rumi.[39] It is like the king or queen of the inner realm. And its desire is for love. This capacity for love in us is the greatest strength of our being and the deepest delight of our souls. So, "gamble everything for love," says Rumi. There is no room here for "half-heartedness".[40] Seek it with all that you are. Let go of your hesitations.

> Don't go to sleep one night.
> What you most want will come to you then.
> Warmed by a sun inside, you'll see wonders.
> Tonight, don't put your head down.
> Be tough, and strength will come.
> That which adoration adores
> appears at night. Those asleep
> may miss it …
> … The day is for work
> The night is for love.
> … Some people sleep at night.
> But not lovers. They sit in the dark
> and talk to God …
> This moment is all there is.
> Death will take it away soon enough.
> You'll be gone, and this earth will be left
> without … [one of its] sweetheart[s].[41]

Give everything for love. Seek union everywhere with the Beloved. This is the religion of love-madness, not the religion of right behaviour and correct belief. "Theologians mumble, rumble-dumble, necessity and free will," says Rumi, "while lover and beloved pull themselves into each other."[42] They simply get on with the true work of religion, moving back into oneness with the heart of all things.

If you want to know how Jesus raised the dead, says Rumi, just remember what it was like when your lover first kissed you on the lips. Love has the power to awaken our whole being. You all know what love can do, says Rumi. "Your father and mother were playing love games. They came together, and you appeared!"[43] So, don't ask what love can do. Look at the colours of the world. Look at you!

Rumi invites us again and again to remember that love is the true religion:

> Like the ground turning green in a spring wind.
> Like birdsong beginning inside the egg.
> Like this universe coming into existence,
> the lover wakes, and whirls
> in a dancing joy,
> then kneels down
> in praise.[44]

Let go of everything that is not love. This will be the rebirth of true religion.

✷

"I will search for the ... [Beloved] with all my passion and all my energy," says Rumi, "until I learn that I don't need to search."[45] For the love we are longing for is here and now, at the heart of this moment and every moment. "Lovers don't finally meet somewhere," says Rumi. "They're in each other all along."[46] So, when we do awaken to love, says Rumi, it is as if "we've come into the presence of the one who was never apart from us."[47] It is to remember what we've forgotten, the light of the divine at the heart of all things. As the Quran says, "You have but to remember and you will see the light" (The Heights 7.201).

Love is the wine of remembrance. We can be part of helping one another awaken to it. For we and all things live in "love's sanctuary", as Rumi calls this world.[48] It is here and now, "cash in hand".

MEDITATIVE PRACTICE: SEEKING LOVE

Jalaluddin Rumi is a messenger of love to us. He invites us to rediscover it as the true essence of religion, and to rebuild our world as a sanctuary of love in which to honour each other and find delight together. When the grape skin of our ego breaks, the rich wine of love flows in us again for Earth and one another.

(pause to listen for what Rumi's wisdom stirs in us)

As a lover longs for the presence of her beloved
so my soul longs for the body of Earth
and the beauty of the human spirit
that in thought and word and deed each day
in the costly name of love
we may live and move as one again
in the place where the two worlds touch.

(pause to be aware)

As a lover longs for the presence of her beloved
so my soul longs to love.

PART THREE

Seven

Seeking Wisdom: Rabindranath Tagore

I believe in a spiritual world – not as anything separate from this world – but as its innermost truth."[1] So wrote Rabindranath Tagore (1861–1941), Indian poet, Nobel Laureate, and "dreamer of dreams" as he later described himself in his call to the world to rediscover its oneness.[2]

For Tagore it is wisdom that accesses the inner realm of truth. Knowledge, on the other hand, gains entry only into the outer chamber of truth and the physicalness of the world, such as knowing what the constituent elements of the universe are or the neurological workings of the brain. But it is wisdom that enters the spiritual world deep in this world. This is the world that is "old," says Tagore, "and yet ever new."[3] And it is the realm of truth in which we will find our way back into harmony again.

The Western world has been characterized by the outward pursuit of knowledge, along with its practical applications. This has led to scientific discoveries and immense technological advances for humanity. The Eastern world, on the other hand, has been more rooted in wisdom's unitive way of seeing, remembering the oneness of the divine and the human, the kinship of humanity and Earth, and the interrelationship of all things. Tagore is a messenger to us of wisdom's unitive vision of reality at a time when humanity's lack of oneness with Earth and itself threatens to undo us.

Tagore was born in Kolkata into a Brahmin family, the highest of castes in Hindu society, traditionally associated with priestly roles and spiritual wisdom. As well as caring for his family's vast ancestral estates in Bengal, he was a playwright, composer, painter and social reformer. But, first and foremost, he was a poet, articulating a vision of the spiritual world at the heart of this world.

In 1912 Tagore translated into English his Bengali collection of poems entitled *Gitanjali*. He described them as song offerings to God, whom he addresses as the Heart within our heart, the Soul within our soul, and the Light within all life. His translation found its way into the hands of the Irish poet William Butler Yeats, who was deeply stirred by Tagore's poetry. Along with a few other literary figures in Europe, including Ezra Pound, Yeats secured a limited publication for the work in English. The next year it won the Nobel Prize for Literature, despite Tagore's claim that he was deficient in English, so much so that "if anybody wrote an English note asking me to tea," he said, "I never felt equal to answering it."[4] Two years later he was knighted by King George V. The "Bard of Bengal", as he was known, was now a poet of humanity.

These honours in Europe opened the door internationally for Tagore. Invitations flooded in from all over the world. Although he was in his early fifties when he was awarded the Nobel Prize and was the first non-European to win it in the field of literature, over the next three decades he visited thirty-seven countries on five continents. "The world has received me with open arms," he said. "I want to do the same with the world."[5] But it was a demanding transition for a man whose soul had been fed especially by his communion with nature in the Bengali countryside of his family's history. "The winter sun is sweet," he wrote during one of his visits home, "the green is luxuriant all around me. I want to be gloriously idle and let my thoughts melt and mingle in the blue of space. I am beginning even to envy the birds that sing and gladly go without honour."[6]

Tagore had come to see, however, that his newly acquired international role was the great calling of his life. "I realised that my mission was the mission of the present age. It was to make the meeting of the

East and the West fruitful in truth."[7] He saw that Europe was "like a child ... looking out for her mother."[8] Humanity's spiritual awareness had been born in the East. Now the time had come for its wisdom to be shared more deeply and broadly with the rest of the world. "It is exhausting to be so much on the move," he wrote from Los Angeles in October 1916. "But I am willing because it is God's will that I bring my message here. That is why God has steered my boat to these shores without prior notice. I accept His will."[9]

Through Tagore, India's wisdom was now flowing to the West in new ways. And of special significance for Tagore was to share the East's sense of kinship with the natural world. "In India it was in the forests that our civilisation had its birth," said Tagore.[10] The elements of earth, air, fire and water were seen not simply as physical phenomena. They were embodiments of spirit. "The mysteries of the inarticulate rocks, the rushing waters and the dark whispers of the forest" infused India's sense of relationship with the cosmos.[11] And that is why India chose her sites of pilgrimage in places of special grandeur and beauty in nature, rather than simply in terms of human and historical significance. Western civilization, on the other hand, was the product of a "city-wall" mentality, empire-based rather than nature-based.[12] The natural world was viewed as hostile, a realm that had to be subdued to prise from Earth the fruits and harvests of her resources. Europe's invasion of the Indian subcontinent, like its invasion of North America, approached the primeval forests of these lands as sources of wealth and power rather than as "great living cathedrals" in which the soul of humanity could be renewed in contact with the soul of Earth.[13] Tagore saw clearly that when humanity falls out of spiritual relationship with the natural world it creates "bewildering problems" for itself and for the future well-being of Earth.[14]

Tagore also saw that it was important for the West to be reminded that Christianity had its origins in the East. In keeping with Eastern wisdom and its sense of humanity's union with the divine, Jesus speaks of his oneness with God. Yet Western Christianity has never felt comfortable teaching the essential unity of all things with the divine. Jesus is viewed as an exception to humanity rather than as a manifestation of humanity's true nature. And if Jesus were to show up in the modern Western world, said Tagore, at United States Customs in New York, for instance, he would be refused entry for teaching that the poor are blessed. Or, if he were allowed into the nation, he would possibly be assassinated for teaching that mercy and humility are the true signs of greatness. It is a tragedy, said Tagore, that Christianity has been linked to the might and power of empire and privilege. It has deprived the people of India, and of so many other countries in the world, of "true contact" with the wisdom of Jesus.[15]

This, as we have seen, is one of the central features of the Great Search today, the desire to reverence the wisdom of Jesus rather than simply affirming the Church's teachings about Jesus.

At the heart of Tagore's vision is a seeing of the Infinite within the finite, the divine within the human, and Heaven within Earth. He remembers in his early boyhood glimpsing this union of spirit and matter in everything around him:

> We had a small garden attached to our house; it was a fairyland to me, where miracles of beauty were everyday occurrences. Almost every morning in the early hour of the dusk, I would run out from my bed in a great hurry to greet the first pink flush of the dawn through the shivering branches of the palm trees which stood in a line along the garden boundary, while the grass glistened as the dewdrops caught the earliest tremor of the morning breeze. The sky seemed to bring to me the call of a personal companionship, and all my heart – my whole body in fact – used to drink in at a draught the overflowing light and peace of those

silent hours. I was anxious never to miss a single morning, because each one was precious to me. I had been blessed with that sense of wonder which gives a child his right of entry into the treasure house of mystery in the depths of existence.[16]

Or at night as a boy he would sleep out on the veranda of the family home so that "the stars and I could gaze at each other," he says.[17] And the patter of rain during the night "brought dreams from the fairyland, and mother's voice in the evening gave meaning to the stars."[18]

Tagore is articulating the wisdom of the child, which is the wisdom also of great native traditions throughout the world, and of Eastern spirituality in its origins. It is a wisdom that accesses the spiritual world in this world and does not separate the human voice of love from the harmony of the heavens or the intimacy of a garden in the morning light from companionship with the universe in all its expansiveness.

Tagore's family, although Hindu in its origins, had broken with the mainstream of religious practice long before his birth. He was thus raised in an atmosphere of freedom, as he explains, "freedom from the dominance of any creed that had its sanction in the definite authority of some scripture, or in the teaching of some organized body of worshippers."[19] Tagore thus anticipated the large-scale exile from organized religion that many of us are experiencing today and the yearnings to know the presence of the divine deep within the natural world and in the so-called ordinary occurrences and relationships of daily life.

What *did* continue in the Tagore family from their Indian religious inheritance, however, was the practice of meditation. He remembers as a boy watching his father in morning prayer. "The sun had not yet risen," says Tagore, "and he sat on the roof, silent as an image of white stone, his hands folded on his lap."[20] And often he would meditate this way for hours on end. This was to become Tagore's custom too. "At a certain time, the sky in front of my eastern door gradually gets lighter," he says, "and a bird or two begins to twitter; the clouds are touched by a hint of gold ... Immediately I get up. I wash my face and say my prayers on the stone seat in my east veranda. The sun slowly climbs up and blesses me with its rays."[21] And all of this happens in the context of the living cathedral of the natural world. "'Be still, my heart," as Tagore writes in one of his poems, "these great trees are prayers."[22]

The intimations of a light shining in all things that came to him in boyhood were confirmed for Tagore in a visionary experience of early adulthood:

> It was morning. I was watching the sunrise from Free School Lane [in Kolkata]. A veil was suddenly withdrawn, and everything became luminous. The whole scene was one of perfect music – one marvellous rhythm. The houses in the street, the men moving below, the little children playing, all seemed part of one luminous whole – inexpressibly glorious. The vision went on for seven or eight days ... and I was full of gladness, full of love, for every person and every tiniest thing.[23]

During this lifting of the veil, as he described it, "no person or thing in the world seemed trivial". He was experiencing the joy of seeing the Infinite within the finite. And he knew himself and all things suffused by "the world-filling light", as he called it, or the immanence of the divine in all things.[24]

Years later, Tagore described his religion as "a poet's religion" rather than that of "an orthodox man of piety" or a "theologian".[25] It was based on personal experience and vision rather than religious knowledge and training. This meant, as he frankly admits, "that I cannot satisfactorily answer any questions about evil, or about what happens after death. Nevertheless, I am sure that there have been moments in my experience when my soul has touched the infinite and has become intensely conscious of it through the illumination of joy."[26] He makes no claim to understand religion generally. "But I can say with certainty," he writes, "that there is something that is *living* in me. It is a feeling of mystery, not a dogma."[27]

This something that is living in him Tagore calls "the God-within-me".[28] And he looks for this presence everywhere. God is "the Eternal Person manifested in all persons," he says.[29] God is the Soul within all souls. And one of the deepest prayers that has ever arisen from the human heart, says Tagore, finds expression in the Vedic scriptures of Hinduism, "O thou self-revealing one, reveal thyself in me."[30] Show your infinite Self in my self, your eternal Life in my life. Tagore is thus able to speak of the divinity of our humanity and the humanity of our divinity. They are one in us. This is the true purpose of religion, he says, when it touches the divine in our depths, awakening us to our spiritual nature. "Otherwise, it has no justification to exist."[31] For it no longer illumines in us an awareness of our true depths. Nor can it enlighten in us a sacred consciousness of Earth and all life.

For Tagore, it is particularly an awareness of God in those who are "poorest, lowliest, and lost" that true religion awakens in us. Thus, he writes:

> Leave this chanting and singing and telling of beads! Whom dost thou worship in this lonely dark corner of a temple with doors all shut? Open thine eyes and see thy God is not before thee! He is there where the tiller is tilling hard ground and where the path-maker is breaking stones. He is with them in sun and in shower, and his garment is covered with dust. Put off thy holy mantle and even like him come down on the dusty soil! … Come out of thy meditations and leave aside thy flowers and incense! What harm is there if thy clothes become tattered and stained? Meet him and stand by him in toil and the sweat of thy brow.[32]

The same awareness of the divine that Tagore is alert to within himself and all people, regardless of caste or status, he experiences, as we have seen, in the natural world around him. The Infinite is to be seen "in the sunlight, and the green of the earth, in the flowing streams, in the gladness of springtime, the repose of a winter morning" as well as "in the beauty of a human face and the wealth of human love".[33] Within all things, he says, is "a living presence".[34] It is "the Being who manifests one essence in a multiplicity of forms".[35] It is "woven in wondrous mysteries of curves" through the body of Earth, "casting away all barren lines of straightness".[36] To a "God-conscious" person, says Tagore, the "object of worship is present everywhere".[37] The universe is a living temple of the divine.

It was this vision of the divine in the natural world and in every person that shaped Tagore's approach to his education initiative at Shantiniketan in West Bengal. There he offered schooling to children of Muslim families and Hindu families and to the children of villagers working the lands of his family estates. "Children are in love with life," he said.[38] So, the purpose of education is to nurture that love, setting free in the child a creative unity of truth – physically, mentally and spiritually. Whenever possible, the teaching at Shantiniketan occurred outside, under the trees or under the open skies in the living cathedral of the natural world. It is a "strange environment" that humanity has created in the modern world, said Tagore, so often "drawing curtains", as it were, to obstruct our vision of nature. It is a wonder, he said, that we have not yet raised marquees above us at night to "hide the moon" from sight.[39]

In addition to providing the students of Shantiniketan with a natural context for learning, along with simple living and a great latitude of freedom for individual students to follow their intuitions and natural preferences of study, Tagore resisted the practice of textbook learning that was typical of the Indian educational system at the time under the governance of the British Raj. One of his short stories, called "The Parrot's Training", is a caricature of the education system imposed on India by the British.[40]

"Once upon a time there was a bird," begins the story. "It was ignorant. It sang all right, but never recited scriptures. It hopped pretty frequently but lacked manners." So, it was decided that the bird needed "a sound schooling". Its ignorance, of course, was due to its "natural habitat", so a suitable cage had to be built for the bird. And a magnificent cage it was, gilded and decorated, so much so that people came from far and wide to admire it. Books were purchased and manuscripts piled high to force-feed the bird. "Its throat was so completely choked with leaves from the books that it could neither whistle nor whisper." But still sometimes in the early morning it would flutter its wings in "a reprehensible" sort of way. So, its wings were clipped. And the teachers set about educating the bird, with a textbook in one hand and a strap in the other. When, finally, the bird died, nobody noticed for the longest time. For was it not a good thing to have a quiet bird that didn't hop about uncontrollably?

Tagore himself as a boy had hated the colonial style of education in India. "I felt like a caged rabbit in a biological institute," said Tagore.[41] So, his family allowed him to be tutored largely by his older brother, Hemendranath, who had him swimming in the Ganges and hiking through the hills, studying the art, music and poetry of his choice and imagination, and the geography, history and mathematics of his natural inclination. It was this experience of learning that helped shape Tagore's vision of education at Shantiniketan, with its fourfold foundation of cherishing the individual, the natural, the spiritual and the international. It offered knowledge but above all else it nurtured wisdom and an awareness of the spiritual world at the heart of this world. "Relationship is the fundamental truth of this world of appearance," said Tagore, relationship with the sacred deep within our being and all being.[42]

*

Union with the divine does not have to be achieved. It already exists at the heart of our being as pure gift. We simply need to remove "the obstruction of the self," says Tagore.[43] By this he means we need to harness our ego so that it doesn't get in the way of our soul. The greatest teachers of wisdom, he says, have lived "the life of the soul", not the life of "the self".[44] It is the soul that is our faculty of wisdom, not the self. And the wisdom that our soul accesses is for the well-being of all, not simply for the self, whether that be the individual self or the collective self of our nation or race or species. The ego, swollen with exaggerations, can enslave us, preventing us from seeing the divine in Earth and one another, thus preventing us from serving the divine in all things. Our ego, therefore, needs to be put in the background, as it were, so that we can truly see the essence of life, the spiritual world deep in this world, and the divine presence within every presence.

Tagore quotes Jesus as saying, "It is easier for a camel to go through the eye of a needle than for someone who is rich to enter the kingdom of God" (Luke 18:25). The translation from the original New Testament text more accurately reads "rope" rather than "camel". The words in Greek are almost identical and thus easily confused. The "bulging" ego, says Tagore, cannot enter the realm of inner truth.[45] It is like trying to thread a rope through the eye of a needle. Only the soul in its humility can enter.

Tagore tells the story of a man who wanted to get into the Garden of Bliss. He was prevented, however, by a watchman at the gate who accused him of trying to smuggle his self into the Garden. And, sure enough, it was proved that inside the folds of his garment the man had hidden his self, hoping to sneak it with him into the Garden. But true bliss can be attained only by leaving the self at the gateway to the inner realm.

To say that the ego needs to be left behind at the doorway to spiritual consciousness is not a "negation" of the self, says Tagore. It is rather a "dedication" of the self.[46] For the ego is given to serve the soul in its approach to the inner realm of wisdom rather than trying to slip in itself. It must just wait, as it were, until the soul reemerges from the inner garden of wisdom so that it can dedicate itself to the work of sharing truth for the well-being of the world.

The greatest liberator of the self is love. For when we truly love another, we find our soul "in the highest sense", says Tagore.[47] In other words, we find our true greatness of soul. We are set free from the limitations of ego to enter more deeply into union with the heart of one another and Earth. The boundaries we have placed around ourselves become more flexible. Our friendships become less exclusive, our families more hospitable, and our nations less insular. The self is freed by the way of love. And it is not just love of some, says Tagore, it is love of all. It is "the widening of love", as he calls it.[48] It is the "realising" of the divine in every human being and in every creature.[49] And the more we love the more we are set free. But it is not freedom *from* action. It is freedom *in* action. For love longs to give itself away just as a tree in autumn longs to surrender the ripeness of its fruit, not by compulsion but by desire. Wisdom's consciousness in us, allowing us to see and know the sacredness of Earth and every human being, is given that we may translate it into love, and especially love in action. Otherwise, it wilts. Otherwise, our words and deeds, as well as our dreams and creativities, become captured by the self rather than set free by the soul. And we end up serving only ourselves and not the other, thus endangering our own well-being as well as one another's well-being and Earth's well-being.

Sometimes what love brings into our lives is suffering, an agony of heart that we might otherwise never have known. When someone we love suffers, or when someone we love is taken from us by death, our souls cry out with a pain that puts us in touch with the depths of our being, a place within us that is deeper than self. Tagore calls this essence within us "God", the Soul within our soul. And his poetry and teachings invite us back into relationship with this deepest of places within us.

Tagore's mother died when he was a boy. He lost his wife when she was only thirty. Then he experienced in rapid succession the death of his father, one of his daughters, and his youngest son. And even before these bereavements that came so close together, he had lost his sister-in-law, Kadambari, whom he especially loved. At the age of twenty-five this beautiful and creative spirit took her own life. It was a tragedy that broke Tagore. As he later wrote about these losses, "I realised gradually that life must be seen through the window of death in order to reach the truth."[50] The wisdom that Tagore invites us into comes through love, love in both its joys and its sorrows.

One of Tagore's greatest loves was his love of India. "From infancy," he said, "my communion with the universe has been through India."[51] He cherished her forests, mountains and rivers, as he did her people, culture and spiritual wisdom. And it was this love that brought him close to Mohandas Gandhi, whom he was the first to call *Mahatma*, meaning "Great Soul". In turn Gandhi called him *Gurudev*, which means "Shining Teacher" or "Luminous Guru". They had the deepest of respect for one another even though they pursued different callings in relation to the reshaping of India's nationhood. For Gandhi the focus was political independence from Britain, to be achieved through active nonviolent noncooperation with the Empire. Tagore was in favour of independence for India but his focus, first and foremost, was on a social and spiritual reform of India, to be achieved through education and rural reconstruction.

A critical point in Tagore's relationship with British rule in India was the Amritsar Massacre of 1919. On April 13 a large, peaceful crowd gathered in the Jallianwala Gardens in Amritsar to protest the Rowlatt Act, which had been passed by the Imperial Legislative Council in Delhi enabling imprisonment without trial and indefinite detention for those suspected of revolutionary activity against British rule in India. It is thought there were more than ten thousand people in the Gardens that day. Many of them, however, were not protesters but pilgrims on their way home from the nearby Golden Temple, as well as farmers and merchants who had gathered for an annual trade fair. The Gardens were enclosed on all sides by walls, roughly ten feet high, and there was only one main entrance.

An hour after the protest began, a British brigadier general, Colonel Dyer, arrived with fifty armed troops and two armoured vehicles equipped with machine guns. Without warning the crowd to disperse, he blocked the main entrance and ordered his troops to open fire on the densest section of the crowd. The shooting continued for ten minutes. Trapped, the crowd panicked, and many were trampled to death in the chaos. Others leapt into a well at the heart of the Gardens and were drowned or crushed to death. In total, it is thought that over one thousand people died that day, although the military report estimated it at only two hundred deaths. The British government never apologized for the massacre. One hundred years later it spoke only of its deep regret at the death of so many.

Shocked by the crime, Tagore immediately renounced his knighthood from the British Empire and wrote to the viceroy of India, Lord Chelmsford, "I wish to stand, shorn of all special distinctions, by the side of those of my countrymen who, for their so-called insignificance … suffer degradation not fit for human beings."[52] His words were reported throughout the world. Tagore's protest was a turning point in world awareness of the injustices of British rule in India. It helped mark the beginning of the end of the British Raj.

Tagore didn't in fact live to see an independent India, but when independence did come in 1947, India chose words from Tagore for its national anthem. Significantly, the anthem prays for "the salvation of all people", not just the people of India. Wisdom seeks well-being not just for one people or one nation but for every people and every nation. And India's national anthem ends with the words "Victory to Thee".[53] Not victory simply for India but victory for the God-within-all, the Infinite that appears in all that is finite, the divine at the heart of all life. As Tagore had said, "the world is waiting for a country that loves God and not [merely] herself."⁵⁴

Amid the growing calls for the freedom of India from British domination, Tagore gave himself to supporting this cause but also warning his people of the dangers of nationalism. "When India suffers from injustice," he said, "it is right that we should stand against it." But the responsibility to do so is not simply ours as Indians, he said, it is ours "as human beings".[55] The "egoism of Nation" is as dangerous on a world scale as individual egoism is at the personal level. The cult of nationhood is at the root of war and widespread misery among the nations. "Therefore, my one prayer is," said Tagore, "let India stand for the cooperation of all peoples of the world."[56] It was the nationalism of Britain that had humiliated India, he said. This would not be resolved by yet another nationalism trying to counteract it. Tagore called this "the idolatry of Geography", an absolutizing of boundaries that breeds suspicion and disrespect for those on the other side of the barriers we have artificially created.[57]

Tagore longed for the spiritual unity of humanity. We are to be "world-workers", identifying with the soul of all people, not simply with the soul of our own tribe.[58] "I shall ever seek my compatriots all over the world," he said, not simply in my own nation.[59] "I am determined to plant the seed of world humanity It is the task of my old age to put a stop to national chauvinism."[60] The melody of "world-consciousness" must be the song of the future.[61] Its cadence is interdependence, not simply independence. And it is a song to be sung, not a shout to be screamed in anger. For we are to be "music-makers … the dreamers of dreams", bringing about a future of interrelatedness that we have not yet known.[62]

"The God of humanity has arrived at the gates of the ruined temple of the tribe," said Tagore.[63] And it is not just the temple of the tribe that lies in ruins. It is the temple of nation, or race or religion that will lie in ruins if it remains closed to the sacred presence at the heart of Earth and every people. We are all called to be "twice-born", said Tagore,

Seeking Wisdom: Rabindranath Tagore 145

born first in our own home and nation and then born again to the larger world.[64] This is when our individual self becomes our "world-self".[65] And this is when our soul finds its true home in the soul of humanity and the soul of Earth rather than simply in the soul of our own tribe and people.

Tagore developed an international centre at Shantiniketan for East-West relations. He called it Visva-Bharati, a phrase from a Sanskrit Vedic text which means "where the world meets in one nest".[66] Let our ashram in Shantiniketan, he said, be a place of pilgrimage for the world where "we can mingle without the differences of religion, language and race."[67] Let it be like "a festival of lights … where every race brings its own light."[68] And, for Tagore, a true interrelatedness of all things celebrates the uniqueness of each thing. If the individuality of anything is lost, it is a loss also to the whole world. "The universe," he said, "is ever seeking its consummation in the unique."[69] The "world-song" that we are to sing is not to be separate from the unique song of every individual, every nation, and every race.[70] This is wisdom's integrated vision of oneness. It celebrates the whole and the part as one.

Tagore became frail in his last years and had to let go of much of his "world-worker" work, but he kept listening to the Soul within all souls. "Death, your servant, is at my door," he wrote. "He has crossed the unknown sea and brought your call to my home. The night is dark, and my heart is fearful – yet I shall take up the lamp, open my gates, and bow to him my welcome. It is your messenger who stands at my door. I shall worship him with folded hands and with tears. I shall worship him, placing at his feet the treasure of my heart."[71]

Tagore died on August 7, 1941, at the age of eighty in the upstairs room of the house in Kolkata where he was born. Albert Schweitzer, the great German theologian, said of him, "This completely noble and harmonious thinker belongs not only to his own people but to humanity."[72] For he showed us a world-wisdom that belongs to all human beings and to the whole community of Earth, not simply to one nation, one religion, one race or one species. "At last my day has ended," prayed Tagore, "and now in the evening, I sing my last song to say that I have loved Your world."[73]

MEDITATIVE PRACTICE: SEEKING WISDOM

Rabindranath Tagore is a messenger of wisdom to us. He invites us to let the wisdom that was knitted into us in our mother's womb come forth again in ever-fresh ways, that we may see the infinite world deep in this world and the eternal Soul in every soul. He calls in us to free ourselves from the limitations of self and nation, of religion and race, that we may join the one song, the world-song that is deep in the human soul and the soul of Earth.

(pause to listen for what Tagore's wisdom stirs in us)

As truth longs to be known
so my soul longs for wisdom
that I may see the Sun behind all suns
the Eternal Light in every life
and be a dreamer of dreams in this world
a singer of love's song
ever new and everlasting.

(pause to be aware)

As truth longs to be known
so my soul longs for wisdom.

Eight

Seeking Meaning: Etty Hillesum

On March 9, 1941, a young Jewish woman in Amsterdam began to keep a personal diary during the Nazi occupation of her homeland. Over the next few years, she wrote an account of the sufferings of her people and her own search for meaning. The young woman I am referring to is not Anne Frank, the thirteen-year-old girl who went into hiding with her family in the Netherlands to avoid arrest by the Gestapo. I speak rather of Etty Hillesum, a twenty-seven-year-old woman who recorded her journey of soul amid the horror of what one people can do to another and who, in the middle of such terror, was able to witness to the meaning and even the beauty of life. Anne Frank and Etty Hillesum both died in Nazi concentration camps before the end of the war.

Hillesum saw her diary as part of a "dialogue," as she put it, "with what is deepest inside me, which for the sake of convenience I call God."[1] She began journalling in her third-floor room at 6 Gabriël Metsustraat, which overlooked the main square of Amsterdam with its great concert hall at the one end and the Rijksmuseum at the other, and a skating rink in the middle. "Surrounded by my writers and poets and the flowers on my desk," she said, "I loved life." By the end of the following year, she was in a crowded concentration camp in the northeast of Holland. "And there among the barracks, full of hunted and persecuted people, I found confirmation of my love of life." It was, as she put it, one "meaningful whole".[2]

How did Hillesum find meaning, not only in the relative comfort and safety of her room in Amsterdam but also amid the fear and haunted vulnerability of a concentration camp? "Now I live and breathe through my soul," she said.³ This was the depth within her from which she drew meaning. And this is the depth within us all that her story invites us to find in our search for meaning today, in both the joy and the anguish of life.

*

German forces had invaded the Netherlands on May 10, 1940. Five days later the Dutch government surrendered. Shortly after the Nazi occupation of Holland, the military regime began to persecute Dutch Jews. A national strike was called to resist the persecution and stand in solidarity with the Jewish population, the only mass protest of its kind in the history of German-occupied Europe. It was quickly and brutally suppressed. The leaders of the strike were imprisoned and executed, and the military government intensified its pressure on the Jewish people and on any form of Dutch resistance. Jews were thrown out of their jobs, forbidden to buy in stores frequented by non-Jews, and rounded up into a ghetto in the capital with a view to deporting them eventually to concentration camps in the German-occupied territories of Europe.

Not long before the beginning of her diary in the spring of 1941, Hillesum, who had been earning her living primarily as a tutor in Russian, sought the psychological help of Julius Spier, a Jewish therapist in Amsterdam who had trained under Carl Jung. After three or four sessions with Spier, Hillesum became his assistant, then his intellectual partner and lover. His influence on her at this critical juncture in her life, and in the life of her nation, was considerable, not only intellectually and psychologically but spiritually. It was through Spier that she began to access the spiritual writings of Rainer Maria Rilke and Meister Eckhart, as well as the psychoanalytical thought of Jung. And it was under Spier's influence that she turned more intentionally to the Torah, the Quran and the Bible. "The Bible," as she later said, "is so rugged and tender, simple and wise. And so full of wonderful characters, too."⁴

Her words speak of the fresh eyes with which she, as a secular Jew, began to access the wisdom of scripture, including the radical simplicity of Jesus's teachings. In this she anticipated an important aspect of the Great Search of today, which, as we have already noted, is the desire to learn more deeply of love and compassion through the wisdom of Jesus without the encumbrance of the Church's doctrinal teachings about Jesus. Her readings and reflections were now enabling her more and more to live and breathe through her soul.

But above all else it was Spier's encouragement to meditate and pray that led Hillesum into new depths in her inner life. Spier called it "reposing in oneself". By this he meant a repositioning of the self, a finding of one's true centre, not within the limited confines of the ego but within the depths of the soul. "I repose in myself," says Hillesum. "And that part of myself, that deepest and richest part in which I repose, is what I call 'God'."[5]

In her diary she describes her early days of learning to meditate. "I'll turn inward," she writes, "for half an hour each morning before work, and listen to my inner voice. Lose myself. You could also call it meditation." It isn't enough just to do some physical exercise in the mornings, she says. We are spirit as well as body. So, "half an hour of exercise combined with half an hour of meditation" is what she undertakes. "But it's not so simple," she says, that sort of quiet time. "It has to be learnt. A lot of unimportant inner litter and bits and pieces have to be swept out first. Even a small head can be piled high inside with irrelevant distractions."[6] But more and more she becomes committed to her practice of inner listening. "There is a really deep well inside me," she writes. "And in it dwells God. Sometimes I am there, too. But more often stones and grit block the well, and God is buried beneath. Then He must be dug out again."[7]

Hillesum is entirely transparent in her diary. After all, she saw it primarily as a dialogue with the divine deep within herself rather than something that would ever be published for others to read. And she can be amusing when she describes her distractions from the inner life. "For goodness' sake, stop looking at yourself in the mirror, Etty," she writes. "It must be awful to be very beautiful, for then one would not bother to look further inside, one would be so dazzled by the blinding exterior. Others, too, would respond to the beautiful exterior alone, so that one might actually shrivel up inside altogether. The time I spend in front of the mirror, because I am suddenly caught by a funny or fascinating or interesting expression on this really not particularly pretty face of mine, could surely be spent on better things. It annoys me terribly, all this peering at myself. Sometimes I do find that I am looking pretty, but that's largely because of the dim lighting in the bathroom, and at such moments I can't tear myself away from my likeness and pull faces at myself in the glass, hold my head at all sorts of angles before my enraptured gaze."[8]

And this happens for her not only in the morning when she would prefer to be meditating but also at other points in the day. "Even when I am working," writes Hillesum, "I sometimes have a sudden urge to see my face; then I take my glasses off and look into the lenses. It can be quite compulsive. And I feel very unhappy about it all because I realise how much I still stand in my own way." But she becomes increasingly clear about her desire to get in touch with her "soul" or "essence", as she puts it, "or whatever else you care to call what shines through from within".[9] Dwelling too much on the self rather than the soul, she says, leads to a neglect of "the mighty, eternal current" of life that courses deep through each one of us.[10]

Somewhat unexpectedly for a Jew, Hillesum found herself wanting to kneel in prayer rather than the more traditional Jewish posture of standing and bowing, or even rocking, in prayer. "Last night, shortly before going to bed," she writes, "I suddenly went down on my knees in the middle of this large room, between the steel chairs and the matting [on the floor]."[11] Reflecting on this later, she says, "A desire to kneel down sometimes pulses through my body, or rather it is as if my body had been meant and made for the act of kneeling. Sometimes, in moments of deep gratitude, kneeling down becomes an overwhelming urge, head deeply bowed, hands before my face."[12] But again and again in these early months of meditating and praying in Amsterdam, she realizes she is but a beginner. "I am a kneeler in training," as she describes herself.[13]

"What a strange story it really is," she writes, "my story: the girl who could not kneel. Or its variation: the girl who learnt to pray."[14] For a while, Hillesum finds herself embarrassed about describing this posture of prayer, even though it is only in her diary that she writes these things. It is, she says, "as if I were writing about the most intimate of intimate matters. Much more bashful than if I had to write about my love life. But is there indeed anything as intimate as … [our] relationship to God?"[15] This feeling of bashfulness, however, does not put her off kneeling, for she finds that in prayer she opens to love at a deeper level. "Not the kind of love-de-luxe," she says, "that you revel in deliciously for half an hour, taking pride in how sublime you can feel, but the love you can apply to small, everyday things."[16]

But it was not only to small and everyday things that she applied the love that welled up inside her. It was also to the big and historic things of her day. "The threat grows ever greater," says Hillesum, "and terror increases from day to day." Jews were facing more and more restrictions in work and travel under the Nazi regime, and ever greater numbers were being rounded up into the Jewish Ghetto in Amsterdam. "I draw prayer round me like a dark protective wall," she says, "[and] withdraw inside it as one might into a convent cell and then step outside again, calmer and stronger and more collected again."[17]

The spiritual strength that she finds within her depths sets Hillesum free from being overwhelmed by hatred. "It is the problem of our age," she says. "Hatred of Germans poisons everyone's mind." It is not that a response to evil should be half-hearted or that a denouncing of horrendous wrong should be tame. "But indiscriminate hatred is the worst thing there is," she says. "It is a sickness of the soul." In her diary she describes a thought that had surfaced within her like a young blade of grass thrusting its way through a wilderness of weeds. "If there were only one decent German," she says, "then he should be cherished despite that whole barbaric gang, and because of that one decent German it is wrong to pour hatred over an entire people."[18] Just outside her house in Amsterdam she watched a group of German soldiers training in the square. And she prays, "God, do not let me dissipate my strength, not the least little bit of strength, on useless hatred against these soldiers. Let me save my strength for better things."[19] The only way to truly fight war, she says, is "by releasing, each day, the love that is shackled inside us, and giving it a chance to live."[20]

And she sees that the only place and the only time to give love a chance is here and now, always here and always now rather than in some indefinite future. "But it is all so terribly difficult," she writes, for the way of love calls us to look for the divine not only within ourselves but within the other, including the so-called enemy, to help dig out God not only from the depths of our own being but from the depths of every human being.[21] She calls it "the most essential and the deepest in me hearkening unto the most essential and deepest in the other. God to God."[22] Hillesum finds strength deep in her soul. "A little peace," she says, "a lot of kindness, and a little wisdom – whenever I have these inside me, I feel I am doing well."[23]

On the final day of 1941, which was to be her last full year of living safely in Amsterdam, Hillesum reflects on what has been happening within her and all around her that year. She speaks of having learned to be led not primarily by what is happening on the outside, including the terror of the Nazi occupation of Holland and the growing persecution of her people, but by what wells up from deep within her. "It's still no more than a beginning," she says. "But it is no longer a shaky beginning. It has taken root."[24] Or, as she says elsewhere, "Something in me is growing … Let it flourish."[25] For it is as she lives and breathes through her soul that she accesses meaning and draws spiritual strength for the journey ahead, both for herself and for her Jewish brothers and sisters.

*

By the spring of 1942, Dutch Jews were required to wear the yellow star of David to clearly distinguish them in society and to prevent them from entering certain shops or visiting non-Jewish homes or using trams and public transportation. And, after moving the identifiably Jewish population of Holland into the Amsterdam Ghetto, the military regime declared the provinces to be *judenrein* (free of Jews). The Nuremburg Laws, which had been passed by the Nazi Party in Germany in 1935, were now extended also to the Netherlands. The first of these laws, the Protection of German Blood and German Honour, forbade marriage and sexual relations between Jews and Germans. And the second, the Reich Citizenship Law, decreed that only those of Aryan blood were eligible to be Reich citizens, thus denying the rights of citizenship to the entire Jewish population.

In her diary, Hillesum writes of no longer being allowed to walk along the promenade in Amsterdam. Parks and gardens were forbidden territory to Jews, and they were required to be off the streets by eight o'clock at night. Even the use of bicycles was banned for them. In a letter at this time from her father, who was known for his wry sense of humour, he wrote, "Today we have entered the cycleless age. At least we need fear no longer that our bicycles will be stolen. That is some balm for our nerves. In the wilderness we also had to do without bicycles, for forty long years."[26]

But deeper than any humour in the family about the growing persecution was a deepening realization of what lay ahead of them. "There are few illusions left to us," wrote Hillesum. "Life is going to be very hard. We shall be torn apart, all who are dear to one another. I don't think the time is very far off now. We shall have to steel ourselves inwardly more and more."[27]

Increasingly the entries in her diary are written in the form of prayer. "It is sometimes hard to take in and comprehend, O God, what those created in Your likeness do to each other in these disjointed days," she prays. "But I no longer shut myself away in my room, God, I try to look things straight in the face, even the worst crimes."[28] The answer, she believes, is not to shut down to the "cosmic sadness", as she calls it, that rises from deep within her but to open to it. "You must be able to bear your sorrow," writes Hillesum in addressing herself. "Even if it seems to crush you, you will be able to stand up again, for human beings are strong, and your sorrow must become an integral part of yourself, part of your body and soul … Do not relieve your feelings through hatred, do not seek to be avenged on all German mothers, for they, too, sorrow at this very moment for their slain and murdered sons. Give your sorrow all the space and shelter in yourself that is its due … [For] if you do not clear a decent shelter for your sorrow … then sorrow will never cease in this world and will multiply."[29]

Hillesum sees the path of struggle that lies ahead. "The latest news," she writes, "is that all Jews will be transported out of Holland to Poland. And the English radio has reported that 700,000 Jews perished last year alone, in Germany and the occupied territories. And even if we stay alive, we shall carry the wounds with us throughout our lives. And yet I don't think that life is meaningless. And God is not accountable to us for the senseless harm we cause one another. We are accountable to [God]!"[30]

Still in Amsterdam in the early summer of 1942, and aware of the intensified persecution of her people throughout Nazi-occupied Europe, Hillesum chooses to be attentive also to the beauty of the natural world, of sunrise and the unspeakable gift of every new day. "Sun on the balcony," she writes, "and a light breeze through the jasmine … A new day has dawned … I shall linger another ten minutes with the jasmine … How exotic [it] looks, so delicate and dazzling against the mud-brown walls." She knows that many of her people are ceasing to be truly alive, consumed instead by fear and bitterness and hatred. It isn't that she doesn't understand them. It is simply that she longs for more than fear and bitterness and hatred, and she finds it. "I am with the hungry, with the ill-treated and the dying, every day, but I am also with the jasmine and with the piece of sky beyond my window … When I say, I have come to terms with life, I don't mean I have lost hope. What I feel is not hopelessness, far from it … It is a question of living life from minute to minute and taking suffering into the bargain. And it is certainly no small bargain these days." What matters is how we bear it and fit it into our lives. "I sometimes bow my head under the great burden that weighs down on me … and at the same time feel sure that life is beautiful and worth living and meaningful."[31]

A few weeks later, the jasmine on her balcony loses its blossom in heavy rains and storm. "But somewhere inside me," she writes, "the jasmine continues to blossom undisturbed, just as profusely and delicately as ever it did. And it spreads its scent round the House in which You dwell, O God … I bring You not only my tears and my forebodings on this stormy, grey Sunday morning. I even bring You scented jasmine. And I shall bring You all the flowers I shall meet on my way, and truly there are many of those. I shall try to make You at home always."[32]

In July 1942, through the influence of friends, Hillesum was offered a job in the cultural affairs department of the Jewish Council in Amsterdam, a "soft job", as she described it.[33] As in other occupied countries, the council had been formed at the instigation of the German army to mediate between the Nazi leadership in Holland and the Jewish population at large. The military regime gave orders to the council and then let the council decide how to implement the demands. Members of the council were under the illusion that by negotiation they could save the Jewish population from the worst. The declared purpose of the council was to decide who was fit to be sent away for labour service and who was indispensable at home. But its real purpose was to calm the fears of the panic-stricken Jews of Holland. In this way the council became an instrument in the hands of the Nazis. Hillesum immediately felt that she had done something underhanded in accepting the job as a typist at the Jewish Council. "Like crowding onto a small piece of wood adrift on an endless ocean after a shipwreck and then saving oneself by pushing others into the water and watching them drown. It is all so ugly."[34] And the atmosphere at the council was full of hatred and intrigue, everyone intent merely on trying to save themselves. "Nothing can ever atone for the fact," she wrote, "that one section of the Jewish population is helping to transport the majority out of the country. History will pass judgment in due course."[35] One week after starting her work at the Jewish Council, Hillesum volunteered to accompany the first deportation of Jews from Amsterdam. As she wrote in her diary, "I have matured enough to assume my destiny, to cease living an accidental life."[36] She was choosing rather to live a meaningful life, to be in touch with the divine deep within herself and to share the journey of her people in their time of suffering.

The Nazi regime wanted eventually to concentrate the Jewish population in Westerbork, a transit camp in the northeast of the Netherlands, not far from the German border. Though not itself an extermination camp, Westerbork would be the last stop before Auschwitz for more than one hundred thousand Dutch Jews. Hillesum chose to travel with the first deportation from Amsterdam and to work in the camp hospital. The Jewish Council granted her a special permit to come and go between Westerbork and Amsterdam, which she chose to do about a dozen times over the next year, often carrying letters and messages with her to Jewish families and Dutch resistance groups in Holland. And on return she would bring fresh supplies of medicine to the camp hospital.

Westerbork had been built by the Dutch government before the war to house some fifteen hundred German Jews who had fled to the Netherlands for safety. But after the Nazi occupation of Holland, it was revamped as a transit camp. Within a few months of Hillesum's arrival, the camp population swelled to more than ten thousand, and eventually to as many as forty thousand. Every Monday an empty train pulled into the camp, and every Tuesday the long line of freight cars pulled out again, packed with more than a thousand men, women, children and infants for the three-day journey to Auschwitz. "When the first transport passed through our hands [at Westerbork]," wrote Hillesum, "there was a moment when I thought I would never again laugh and be happy, that I had changed suddenly into another, older person cut off from all former friends. But on walking through the crowded camp, I realised again that where there are people, there is life."[37] And every evening she would go to watch the sun setting over the purple lupins behind the barbed wire. She was finding beauty, even amid the suffering that surrounded her.

But "my heart is a floodgate for a never-ending tide of misery," she wrote.[38] "At night, as I lay in the camp on my plank bed, surrounded by women and girls gently snoring, dreaming aloud, quietly sobbing and tossing and turning, women and girls who often told me during the day, 'We don't want to think, we don't want to feel, otherwise we are sure to go out of our minds,' I was sometimes filled with an infinite tenderness, and lay awake for hours letting all the many, too many impressions of a much-too-long day wash over me, and I prayed, 'Let me be the thinking heart of these barracks.' And that is what I want to be … the thinking heart of a whole concentration camp."[39] But it was especially the babies, "those tiny piercing screams of the babies," dragged from their cots in the middle of night in preparation for the Tuesday morning transport that was almost too much to bear.[40] "A name occurs to me," she wrote, "Herod."[41] Although Hillesum didn't yet know exactly what awaited them in Auschwitz, she knew there was no coming back. She realized that she was witnessing in her own time the unfolding story of the slaughter of the innocents.

"I have looked our destruction, our miserable end, which has already begun in so many small ways … straight in the eye and accepted it into my life," writes Hillesum, "and my love of life has not been diminished."[42] Much of this love of life in Hillesum, even at Westerbork, was her love of the women and men and children who surrounded her. "I love people so terribly," she says, "because in every human I love something of You [O God]. And I seek You everywhere in them and often do find something of You."[43]

"But one thing is becoming increasingly clear to me," she prays, "that You cannot help us, that we must help You to help ourselves. And that is all we can manage these days and also all that really matters: that we safeguard that little piece of You, God, in ourselves ... We must help You and defend Your dwelling place inside us to the last."[44]

Hillesum's sense of the divine was not an all-powerful transcendent being who could somehow be held responsible for the unjust sufferings of her people and who, if she only prayed hard enough, might intervene to save the innocent, and punish the oppressors. For her the divine was that deepest presence of love within us that will never be undone by hatred or violence or war and is the only source of peace. "I ... believe," she said, "childishly perhaps but stubbornly, that the earth will become more habitable again only through the love that the Jew Paul described to the citizens of Corinth in the thirteenth chapter of his first letter":[45]

> If I speak in the tongues of mortals and of angels, but do not have love, I am a noisy gong or a clanging cymbal.
>
> And if I have prophetic powers, and understand all mysteries and all knowledge, and if I have all faith, so as to remove mountains, but do not have love, I am nothing.
>
> If I give away all my possessions, and if I hand over my body so that I may boast, but do not have love, I gain nothing.
>
> Love is patient; love is kind; love is not envious or boastful or arrogant or rude. It does not insist on its own way; it is not irritable or resentful; it does not rejoice in wrongdoing but rejoices

in the truth.

It bears all things, believes all things, hopes all things, endures all things.

Love never ends.

(I Cor. 13:1–8)

"I shall merely try to help God as best I can," she says, "and if I succeed in doing that, then I shall be of use to others as well. But I mustn't have heroic illusions about that either."[46]

Her calling, from day to day, and from minute to minute, was simply to be attentive to the presence of the divine within herself and within others and try to be faithful to that as best she could. "Sometimes I might sit down beside someone [in the camp]," she says, "put an arm round a shoulder, say very little and just look into their eyes ... And at the end of each day, there was always the feeling: I love people so much."[47]

During the months when Hillesum was free to travel back and forth between Westerbork and Amsterdam, she refused all attempts by her Amsterdam friends to take her to a safe house, on one occasion even by force. "I don't think I would feel happy if I were exempted from what so many others have to suffer," she wrote. "They keep telling me that someone like me has a duty to go into hiding, because I have so many things to do in life, so much to give. But I know that whatever I may have to give others, I can give it no matter where I am."[48]

✻

Hillesum made the journey from Amsterdam to Westerbork for the last time in June 1943. For many months, she had been seeing that "what is at stake," as she put it, "is our impending destruction and annihilation. We can have no more illusions about that. They are out to destroy us completely."[49] It is unlikely she would have heard of the "Final Solution", as it was called, the official Nazi code name for the deliberate and systematic genocide of the Jewish people, beginning across German-occupied Europe and extending into any territories that might yet be seized by the Third Reich. Hillesum may not literally have heard of the "Final Solution" but she was sensing it and witnessing it unfold before her very eyes.

"I want to live to see the future," she says, and to write an account of what is happening now.[50] "'I shall wield this slender fountain pen as if it were a hammer, and my words will have to be so many hammer strokes with which to beat out the story of our fate and of a piece of history as it is and never was before. A few people must survive … if only to be the chroniclers of this age. I would very much like to become one of their number."[51] And Hillesum repeatedly wishes that she could write more poetically, to powerfully express her sense of both the beauty and suffering of life. But "there is no hidden poet in me," she writes, "just a little piece of God that might grow into poetry."[52]

"The misery here is quite terrible," she writes, "and yet, late at night when the day has sunk away into the depths behind me, I often walk with a spring in my step along the barbed wire. And then time and again, it soars straight from my heart – I can't help it, that's just the way it is, like some elementary force – the feeling that life is glorious and magnificent, and that one day we shall be building a whole new world. Against every new outrage and every fresh horror, we shall put up one more piece of love and goodness, drawing strength from within ourselves. We may suffer, but we must not succumb. And if we should survive unhurt in body and soul, but above all in soul, without bitterness and without hatred, then we shall have a right to a say after the war. Maybe I am an ambitious woman: I would like to have just a tiny bit of say."[53]

Shortly after her return to Westerbork in June 1943, Hillesum experienced what she called "the hardest day" of her life. "The jam-packed freight train [from Amsterdam] drew into the camp this morning," she wrote. "I stood beside it in the rain. The cars were shut tight, but there were a few small openings here and there high up, where the planks had been broken. Through one of these I suddenly spotted Mother's hat and Father's glasses and Mischa's peak face." Her mother and father, and her youngest brother, had finally been deported. Mischa was a brilliant musician, considered by many to be one of the most promising pianists in Europe. As part of a supposed elite of artists, Dutch officials had offered him a relatively safe place at Schaffelaar Castle in Barneveld, Holland, meant for "cultural Jews". But he declined unless his parents could accompany him. So instead, they were deported together to Westerbork. "Soon I'll have to take them to the large barracks," writes Hillesum, "where all hell has been let loose. I don't think there are even enough beds for everyone, and there are no mattresses for the men."[54]

Hillesum now struggles like never before not to be paralysed by fear, especially for her parents. The only attitude that allows one to carry on at Westerbork, she writes, is derived from St. Matthew's Gospel, "Do not worry about tomorrow, for tomorrow will bring worries of its own. Today's trouble is enough for today" (Matt. 6:34). We must not respond to the evil of today with fear for tomorrow and hatred of those who wrong us. Our only duty is "to reclaim large areas of peace in ourselves, more and more peace, and to reflect it towards others."[55] That, she says, is "the only solution".[56] And that, rather than the so-called Final Solution, is the only way forward for humanity.

On July 5, 1943, Hillesum's status with the Jewish Council, along with her freedom to travel, was suddenly revoked. She was now simply a camp internee at Westerbork with more than thirty thousand other prisoners. She knew now that it was no longer a question of living but of how to prepare for death. Around this time, she wrote to her dear friend Maria, "How terribly young we were only a year ago on this heath! Now we've grown a little older. We hardly realise it ourselves; we have become marked by suffering for a whole lifetime. And yet life in its unfathomable depths is so wonderfully good."⁵⁷

Although she continued for some time to be able to send letters from Westerbork, the final words of her diary were, "We should be willing to act as a balm for all wounds."⁵⁸ Not only the wounds of those immediately around us but the wounds of humanity. "If we were to save only our bodies and nothing more from the camps all over the world, that would not be enough. What matters is not whether we preserve our lives at any cost, but how we preserve them … If we have nothing to offer a desolate post-war world but our bodies saved at any cost, if we fail to draw new meaning from the deep wells of our distress and despair, then it will not be enough."⁵⁹

Hillesum believed that the only way of truly preparing for a new world is by living it now in our hearts. And she knew that deep in her soul was a strength to be able to do that. "You have made me so rich," she prayed, "please let me share out Your beauty with open hands. My life has become an uninterrupted dialogue with You, O God, one great dialogue … The beat of my heart has grown deeper, more active, and yet more peaceful, and it is as if I were all the time storing up inner riches."⁶⁰ I feel "full of strength and love," she says. "I would so much like to help prepare the new age."⁶¹

Two months after Hillesum's special status was revoked, her name appeared without prior notice on the weekly transport list, along with her parents and brother. On the morning of September 7, they were packed with a thousand other inmates onto the Westerbork train bound for Auschwitz. Hillesum wrote a final note and threw it out of the train. It was a postcard addressed to her friend Christine van Nooten. Dutch farmers found it in a field and posted it on to Amsterdam. "Opening the Bible at random I find this," wrote Hillesum, 'The Lord is my high tower.' I am sitting on my rucksack in the middle of a full freight car. Father, Mother, and Mischa are a few cars away. In the end, the departure came without warning. On sudden special orders from The Hague. We left the camp singing."⁶² On the same day, Jopie Vleeschhouwer, a friend from Westerbork, wrote a letter to Etty's circle of friends in Amsterdam describing her departure from the camp:

> She stepped onto the platform … talking gaily, smiling, a kind word for everyone she met on the way, full of sparkling humour, perhaps just a touch of sadness, but every inch the Etty you all know so well … I only wish I could describe for you exactly how it happened and with what grace she and her family left! … Mischa waved through a crack in wagon no. 1, [then there was] a cheerful "bye" from Etty in no. 12, and they were gone. She is gone. We stand bereft, but not with empty hands.[63]

The journey lasted three days. They reached Auschwitz on September 10. That very day, her mother and father were gassed as were the majority who had travelled with them from Westerbork, including children and infants. At this point in the war, up to twenty thousand people were being murdered every day at Auschwitz, primarily Jews, but also Roma, Black people, homosexuals, those with mental or physical disabilities, and anyone else whom the "master race" considered impure and degenerate. Those capable of work were spared for the time being. Hillesum and her brother were registered at the so-called Gate of Death in Auschwitz, tattooed on their left arms with serial numbers, stripped, shaved, given prison uniforms, designated "Jude" with the yellow star of David on their shirts, and forced into labour under harrowing conditions.

The Nazis finally murdered Hillesum at Auschwitz on November 30, 1943, and her brother Mischa the following year. Her other brother, Jaap, who for some time had been allowed to remain in Amsterdam to continue his work as a medical doctor, was eventually sent to Bergen-Belsen, a concentration camp in northern Germany, where he survived the war but died on his return journey to Holland. Her entire family was lost, as were two-thirds of the Jewish population of Europe, almost six million women, men, and children.

Hillesum's diary, which she gave to a friend in Amsterdam before her last journey to Westerbork, was published almost forty years after her death, and finally appeared in English in 2002. She did indeed become a chronicler of her people's story, to have a say in how a new world might be built. The most repeated refrain in her diary, both from the Amsterdam years and from Westerbork, was "life is beautiful and meaningful". And this is what she invites us into, in our living and our dying, and in times of joy as well as sorrow, to know that life is an unspeakably beautiful gift, forever graced with meaning when we live and breathe from our true depths and listen for the divine at the heart of our being.

MEDITATIVE PRACTICE: SEEKING MEANING

Etty Hillesum is a messenger of meaning to us. She invites us to live and breathe through our souls to access the meaning of life in both its glory and agony. She inspires us to defend the dwelling place of the divine deep within us and all life, and to know in our hearts the strength of love to bear all things, hope all things, and endure all things.

(pause to listen for what Hillesum's wisdom stirs in us)

As the mind longs to understand
so my soul yearns for meaning
in both the beauty and pain of life
in the yellow blossoming of jasmine at my window
and its scent in the garden of my soul
in the fears of those who call out at night
and their dread of the journey ahead.
May I find the strength to endure
and witness to the coming of a new day.

(pause to be aware)

As the mind longs to understand
so my soul yearns for meaning.

Nine

Seeking Faith: Edwin Muir

The term "loss of faith" has been applied to the modern world, especially in its response to the meaningless suffering caused by war, injustice and environmental neglect. Why must the innocent suffer? For countless numbers of people, traditional religious belief has failed the test. It has neither lessened the suffering nor addressed it in ways that might reverse the deep spirals of wrong.

The Scottish poet Edwin Muir (1887–1959) was one among many who lost faith early in the twentieth century. In this he anticipated the seismic collapse of religion that characterizes a modern nation like Scotland and so many other parts of the Western world today. In Muir's case it was precipitated by the deaths of four members of his family within a few years, as well as the experience of poverty and human degradation in the heavily industrialized city of Glasgow. Muir eventually came to see, however, that what he had lost was not faith in God but faith in what the church had taught him about God and humanity and Earth.

For Muir, the journey back was a long one. And, as we shall see, it was not simply a return to traditionally held religious belief. It was an imaginative reclaiming of his first vision of reality as a child in which he experienced the universe as flooded with light. Faith for him was about being faithful to the immortal presence that shines in all things. And he also came to see that deep in his Christian inheritance were symbols and myths and wisdom that could serve this faithfulness. This is the recovery of faith that Muir invites us into, and to allow our first experiences of light in nature and in human relationship to be born anew in us and guide us in our living and thinking and acting.

*

Muir was born in the Orkney Islands, to the north of the Scottish mainland where the Atlantic Ocean and North Sea meet, often in turbulent waters and dangerous crosscurrents. His early childhood was on the small island of Wyre, two miles long and one mile across, with a population of only seven farming families. In his *An Autobiography*, which is like a lens into the human story through the telling of his own story, Muir describes his first memory of light:

> I was lying in some room watching a beam of slanting light in which dusty, bright motes danced and turned ... My mother was in the room, but where I do not know; I was merely conscious of her as a vague, environing presence. This picture is clear and yet indefinite, attached to one summer day at the [farm on Wyre] ... and at the same time to so many others that it may go back to the day when I first watched a beam of light as I lay in my cradle ... The sense of deep and solid peace has come back to me since only in dreams. This memory has a different quality from any other memory in my life. It was as if, while I lay watching that beam of light, time had not yet begun.[1]

Time does not yet exist for us in early childhood, says Muir. It is as if there is only one day "endlessly rising and setting".[2] And the child's eyes are open with wonder to the light that fills the world.

Muir's early childhood was an experience of harmony, not only around him in his sense of the oneness of earth, sea, and sky, but in the natural rhythms and goodness of family life:

> The worst punishment we knew was an occasional clip across the ears from my father's soft cap ... and this never happened

unless we were making an unbearable noise. Afterward he would sit back looking ashamed ... My mother had more practical sense than my father but was just as gentle.[3]

Part of the natural rhythm of family life in Muir's childhood was the ritual of Sunday observance on the island. There was no church on Wyre, so on Sunday mornings the people would set out together in their boats to cross the narrow stretch of sea to the next island, although often the weather was too rough to risk the journey. But always on a Sunday there was a special meal of soup with chicken cooked in it to celebrate the Sabbath. Shining spoons and knives and forks were laid out on the white tablecloth. "During the week," he writes, "we did not bother much about knives and forks and tablecloths." A big plate of fish was set in the middle of the table alongside a dish of potatoes, and everyone simply stretched out their hands into the common bowl. The traditional Orkney invitation to a visitor was, "Put in thee hand." It was a simple act of communion.[4]

Muir's father was a religious man but not strict or ostentatious in his piety:

> He often omitted grace before meals for long stretches; then he would remember and begin again. Every Sunday night he gathered us together to read a chapter of the Bible and kneel down in prayer. These Sunday nights are among my happiest memories; there was a feeling of complete security and union among us as we sat reading about David or Elijah. My father's prayer, delivered in a sort of mild chant while we knelt on the floor, generally ran on the same lines; at one point there always came the words, for which I waited, "an house not made with hands, eternal in the heavens."[5]

This sense of spiritual well-being was lost for Muir when he moved with his family from the Orkney Islands to the crowded, industrialized city of Glasgow. But even in his early childhood there were signs of a religious way of seeing that would not stand the test of time for Muir. In the family home on Wyre, for instance, there was a children's Bible storybook that was written and illustrated in a tone of sentimental piety. "It gave me the impression," said Muir, "that Jesus was always slightly ill … with the special gentleness of people who cannot live as others do."[6]

Much more appealing to Muir was the experience of meeting the mighty workhorses when his father would lead them from the fields into the courtyard of the farm. "Everything about them, the steam rising from their soft leathery nostrils, the sweat staining their hides, their ponderous irresistible motion … the waterfall sweep of their manes, the ruthless flick of their cropped tails, the plunge of their iron-shod hoofs striking fire from the flagstones, filled me with terror and delight … I loved and dreaded them as an explorer loves and dreads a strange country which he has not yet entered."[7]

Muir was always attracted to the robust and elemental energies of the natural world in his sense of what is real and true spiritually. And later in life he was critical of the way Western Christianity had turned the Incarnation into a religious idea that focused limitedly on Jesus rather than expressing the primal embodiment of the divine in Earth and humanity. In his poem "The Incarnate One", in which he imagines sitting in an austere Scottish Presbyterian church in the north of Scotland with no furnishings other than its hard wooden pews and raised central pulpit, Muir writes, "And the Word made flesh is here made Word again."[8] He is describing a way of seeing in which the Incarnation becomes a creedal statement of belief about the divine rather than looking for it in the colours, textures and forms of Earth and the human mystery. It was a religious teaching that treated Jesus as an exception to humanity rather than as a manifestation of what is deepest in every human being and every life-form.

Even as a boy Muir resisted unnaturalness and affectation in religious practice and behaviour. At the age of fourteen he experienced "conversion" at a revivalist meeting in the town of Kirkwall on the mainland of Orkney. At the end of the sermon, in response to an invitation to personally accept God into his life, the young Muir had been swept to his feet by the religious fervour of the congregation and followed others to the front of the church to kneel at the altar rail:

> The preacher asked me to offer up a prayer, but I could not think of one, and felt that it would be presumptuous of me, so newly converted, to address God out of my own invention. Beside me was kneeling a red-haired, spectacled young man who ... now burst into a loud and rapid prayer, as if he were already resolved to make a record in the world of the saved. My exaltation did not keep me from feeling slightly annoyed with him for his forwardness; but I suppressed the feeling, telling myself that I must love him.[9]

Muir soon doubted his conversion experience. He had not really known what he was doing, despite the earnest enthusiasm of those around him. But any change that he felt in his heart that day did not last long. Later that same year, his father's health failed. The farm had to be given up, and the family moved to Glasgow, "a terrible mistake," said Muir.[10] In the winter of 1901, they headed south to the most overcrowded, slum-infested city of Britain. In two days, as he later put it, they covered more than one hundred and fifty years. They had journeyed from pre-industrialized Orkney, where life had remained pretty much the same for hundreds of years, to the heavily industrialized city of Glasgow, cut off from nature and dominated by economic forces of competition and survival. "Slum grass, scabbed and aching trees, and desecrated ground," said Muir, "a feeling of blasphemy."[11]

Muir's boyhood faith failed him in his transition to Glasgow. Within two years, four members of the family had died, his father and mother, and two of his brothers. Traditional religious belief provided him with no comfort or meaning at this critical juncture in his life. If the Orkney years had been a Garden of Eden to Muir, the move south was an experience of the Fall. And, as he later put it in one of his poems, life was "smashed to bits by the Fall".[12]

Muir's schooling also ended now, for he had to work to help support the remaining members of the family. To begin with he found employment as an office boy in the city. "I walked to and from my work each day through a slum," he said. "These journeys filled me with a sense of degradation: the crumbling houses, the twisted faces, the obscene words casually heard in passing, the ancient, haunting stench of pollution and decay … daunted me, and at last filled me with an immense, blind dejection."[13]

This now became the norm for Muir over the next two decades, clerical jobs in Glasgow, including work in the office of a bone factory where decaying animal remains were tossed into great furnaces to melt the fat into grease and reduce the bones to charcoal. It was for Muir demeaning work, and he constantly carried on his clothing and body the stench of death and decay from the factory. More and more he felt cut off from his beginnings in Orkney and from his own true depths. "Something in me was buried," he wrote, "and I was only half there as I worked in the office … I felt that I had gone far away from myself."[14]

Although his formal education had ceased, Muir was a voracious reader and a bright, inquiring mind. He increasingly turned in his inner journey to the writings of the nineteenth-century German philosopher Friedrich Nietzsche, who, as we noted earlier, had famously declared that God is "dead". Our hope, therefore, is to be placed solely in the resolve of human willpower and action. This vision of human potential appealed to the young Muir in his loss of religious faith. Nietzsche's thought led him into a type of atheistic socialism that advocated the coming of a new age through the working class's acquisition of political power. It was a heady and strident vision for change that Muir adopted over these years in Glasgow. Although it did something to bring him out of himself and focus his energies on the possibility of society's transformation, it did nothing to address his spiritual depths or reawaken his childhood memories of a light-filled universe. Real change began to come for Muir not through philosophy and political theory but through relationship.

Muir was introduced to Willa Anderson in the winter of 1918 during a visit by her to Glasgow. They met again in the spring of 1919, fell in love, and were married that summer. "In September," wrote Muir, "we both went down to London without a job between us, with very little money, and with hopes over which our sensible friends shook their heads."[15] But his marriage to Willa was the turning point in his life, the beginning of his release from doubt and his many years of despair in Glasgow. As he wrote years later in a poem dedicated to her:

> Yes, yours, my love, is the right human face.
> I in my mind had waited for this long,
> Seeing the false and searching for the true,
> Then found you as a traveller finds a place
> Of welcome suddenly amid the wrong
> Valleys and rocks and twisting roads. But you,
> What shall I call you? A fountain in the waste,
> A well of water in a country dry,
> Or anything that's honest and good, an eye
> That makes the whole world bright. Your open heart,
> Simple with giving, gives the primal deed,
> The first good world, the blossom, the blowing seed,
> The hearth, the steadfast land, the wandering sea,
> Not beautiful or rare in every part,
> But like yourself, as they were meant to be.[16]

In London, Muir now began to get work as a literary reviewer for Scotland's national newspaper *The Scotsman* and other British journals. And, in time, Muir and Willa began a partnership of translating novels from German, including many works by the novelist Franz Kafka. Willa, among the first Scottish women to attend university, had studied German at St. Andrews University, and Muir brought to the partnership a sense of literary style and poetic expression. In their personal lives they addressed one another as "thee" and "thou", the form of intimate speech that Muir reclaimed from his Orkney heritage. And Willa brought to the marriage a great deal of humour and laughter. When their American publisher asked for a description of Muir that could be used in their next publication, this is what she sent him:

> Lived on a small island containing one tree (known as The Tree) ... At the age of fourteen went to Glasgow: saw trains, elevators, and street cars for the first time in his life. Learnt to use a knife and fork, and to wash daily ... [Moved] to London with 60 dollars, abetted by his wife, a reckless woman from the Shetland Islands, with whom he speaks in the barbarous dialect of these regions ...
>
> Gives a general impression of quietness, gentle kindliness, and a little reserve. Black hair, blue eyes, very slim, small hands and feet, looks ridiculously young and won't say how old he is. Has an enormous forehead, like a sperm whale's ... Witty when at his ease: elegant when he can afford it: sensitive and considerate: horribly shy and silent before strangers, and positively scared by social functions. Among friends, however, becomes completely daft, and dances Scottish reels with fervour. Smokes cigarettes continually ... enjoys being petted: and is beloved by cats, dogs, small children, and nearly all women.[17]

Muir's relationship with Willa set him free to open to depths within himself that had long been closed. A few months after arriving in London he entered analysis with a Jungian therapist. It was painful at first as floodgates opened within him and the unconscious came gushing up in the form of powerful dreams and daydreams. But soon he came to see that sleep, and especially the dreams of the night, can take us more deeply into reality if we allow the unconscious to rise into awareness within us. "Sleep," he says, "tells us things both about ourselves and the world which we could not discover otherwise." And it was in sleep, especially in what he calls that "half-discarnate state which precedes and follows sleep", that Muir began to glimpse again the presence of the immortal within himself and all things.[18] As he later wrote in his poem "Day and Night", we need them both, day and night, the conscious and the unconscious, dreaming and wakefulness:

> I wrap the blanket of the night
> About me, fold on fold on fold –
> And remember how as a child …
> I first discovered what is old
> From the night and the soft night wind.
>
> …
>
> The night, the night alone is old
> And showed me only what I knew,
> Knew, yet never had been told;
> A speech that from the darkness grew
> Too deep for daily tongues to say.[19]

In London Muir opens to what he calls "the shepherd of the dark". Again and again in his dreams, he finds himself diving headfirst into unknown depths. Sometimes these depths are limitless. At other times, he sees himself crashing to the ground, and then being reborn from deep within the earth. It is these experiences of the immortal in dream life that begin to lead Muir increasingly to look for the light of the eternal in all things and to remember the glints of immortality he had seen all around him in childhood.

His earliest years in Orkney came alive again in him after having been forgotten for so long. He remembers his "original vision of the world", a light-filled universe, in which "the sky fitted the earth and the earth the sky", everything – humanity, the creatures and the elements – merging in a single flow of interrelationship.[20] It was for Muir like a return to Eden, a spiritual journey of reconnection with the heart of life. The sufferings of family life, and the injustices and wrongs he had witnessed in Glasgow, were not forgotten. But as he put it years later in one of his greatest poems, "One Foot in Eden", despite the blighted and darkened fields of human experience, "yet still from Eden springs the root as clean as on the starting day."[21] He sees that the garden of the eternal is still deep within us, green and good and growing. It has not been undone.

In his dreamlife and memories of childhood, Muir awakens to his true depths. "Remember, remember," as he writes in his diary. "We begin to die when we stop remembering."[22] He realizes it is as if he had been "sleepwalking" for decades, forgetting what at some level he deeply knew within himself. This awakening, he said, was like striking up "a first acquaintance with myself. I did not feel so much that I was rediscovering the world of life as that I was discovering it for the first time."[23] Muir was being born anew.

His work as a literary reviewer, as well as the translating work he shared with Willa, was now financially secure enough to enable them in the summer of 1921 to leave England and spend the next two years living in European cities, including Prague, Dresden, Rome, Salzburg and Vienna. It was during these years that his imagination more and more came back to life, and he began to write poetry, much of which reflects his growing sense of time and eternity intertwined. Increasingly he becomes aware of the immortal at the heart of every moment and every living thing.

In their travels through Europe, the Muirs mingled with artists, writers and musicians from all over the world. In Paris, for instance, they came to know Peggy Guggenheim, an art collector and heiress of the wealthy Jewish Guggenheim family from New York. "I liked Edwin Muir from the very beginning," she wrote, "so sensitive and pure that you could not do otherwise than like him. You felt his talents, even though he … never acclaimed himself. Muir reminded me of a man who has been asleep in front of the fire too long and could not recover from his drowsiness."[24] Well, maybe that is because he was so much in touch with his unconscious depths. But more and more he was waking, not only to the realm of the imaginal but also to the growing social and political discontent of Europe, and the foreboding signs of an anti-semitism that was already rearing its head in Germany and would eventually plunge the world into war again.

In 1924 Muir and his wife returned to Britain, spending time in Scotland to begin with, then back to England to live in Surrey so that they could be close to the publishing world and their literary friends in London. They continued to translate Kafka's novels, and Muir began to publish his poetry as well as his reviews. His voice was beginning to be heard throughout Britain, and by the early 1930s he was frequently being asked to give talks for BBC Radio. Their son Gavin had been born by now and they moved back to Scotland to the university town of St. Andrews.

The experience of family life that he had lost as an adolescent when his parents and two brothers died, Muir now began to recover in his early years of fatherhood. He describes in his diary getting up at half past four one summer morning in St. Andrews so that he and young Gavin could experience the rising of the sun together. The light grew stronger and stronger for us from the east, he says, until "the whole world seemed to be flooded with light … And then, in a few minutes, the sun rose: deep golden yellow, molten, a living fire ... [rising] as if for the first time."[25] He was reliving with his son the grace of a light-filled universe that he had known as a boy in Orkney.

The university town of St. Andrews at times felt overly rarefied for the Muirs, but they formed some close friendships during these years. On Saturdays, for instance, they often shared an evening meal with Oscar Oeser, a lecturer in the Psychology Department, along with his wife, Drury. She describes Muir as a shy, humorous and affectionate man but with a "gentle toughness" about him. "From a woman's point of view," she says, "Edwin was an especially delightful person when he got just a little drunk with wine. Then some of his shyness and inhibitions disappeared, and if one were sitting by him, he would become what I can only describe as chastely affectionate and very beguiling. He would bend towards one from time to time and kiss one, gently, lightly and with leisurely enjoyment, looking slightly mischievous."[26]

But the St. Andrews years were not easy for Muir. The approach of war with Nazi Germany meant there was little demand for the translation of German novels, and Willa had become unwell with an internal bleeding complication that had never properly healed after the birth of Gavin. By February 1939 she was being treated in the hospital. It was at this difficult time that Muir had a spiritual experience that profoundly changed his life. In his diary he writes:

> Last night, going to bed alone, I suddenly found myself (I was taking off my waistcoat) reciting the Lord's Prayer in a loud, emphatic voice – a thing I had not done for many years – with deep urgency and profound disturbed emotion. While I went on, I grew more composed. As if it had been empty and craving and were being replenished, my soul grew still; every word had a strange fullness of meaning which astonished and delighted me. It was late; I had sat up reading; I was sleepy; but as I stood in the middle of the floor half-undressed, saying the prayer over

and over, meaning after meaning sprang from it, overcoming me again with joyful surprise; and I realized that this simple petition was always universal and always inexhaustible, and day by day sanctified human life.[27]

It was now that Muir made the connection between the immortal light that shines in all things and the cherished prayer of his Christian inheritance. He saw that he was born of this Light, the one whom Jesus called "Father". He began to read the New Testament, particularly the Gospels, over and over. "Now I realized," he later wrote in his autobiography, "that, quite without knowing it, I was a Christian, no matter how bad a one."[28] But, for a long time, he was not able to speak about this rebirth of faith within himself for he still lacked words to give it expression.

The following year, however, he wrote to an old friend, saying, "I am happier than I have been, in spite of the state of the world, for I have had something like a sense of the presence of God, a sense which I have never consciously been aware of before, though I am now 52; it is too new and strange for me to write about, and so inexperienced that I am afraid of writing about it … I tremble to lose it again by my own fault. Perhaps I should not have written about it at all, for I cannot tell anything about it, but only so far *feel* it at times."[29]

Muir's faith was always to remain humble, tentative and undogmatic. Perhaps these are the essential features of a recovered faith for today, basing our faith not on the definitive statements of religious tradition but on our deepest and inexpressible experiences of life. As he writes to another friend in 1940, "I have faith [but I cannot accept the doctrines of any Church] … Theological dogmas do not help me; I can't digest them for any good; they're an obstacle to me (perhaps they shouldn't be, but they are); and so I'm a sort of illicit Christian, a gate-crasher, hoping in my own way to slip in."[30]

Although Muir felt ill-equipped to express his faith, he began to weave his sense of the presence of the divine into his poetry. Titles such as "The Fall", "Adam's Dream", "One Foot in Eden", "The Annunciation", "The Incarnate One", and "The Transfiguration" now appear in his published works. And always it is an expression of faith that is rooted in deep human experience rather than the acceptance of religious teachings. "Father Adam and Mother Eve," he says, "teach me, teach me to believe."[31] Significantly, it is not "Mother Church", teach me to believe, but "Mother Eve", teach me to believe. The mysteries of faith that he now points to in his poetry are grounded in his own deepest experiences of life. Immortality is something we can know within us, the shining of an eternal presence. Incarnation is something we can witness in one another and in everything that has being, the sacred essence of every person and every creature. And transfiguration is something we can know at moments of illumination in our lives when our eyes are opened to see again the glory at the heart of life. In his poem "Transfiguration", he writes:

> The source of all our seeing rinsed and cleansed
> Till earth and light and water entering there
> Give back to us the clear unfallen world.

He experiences what he calls the "immortal substance" of all things, and "the unseeable one glory of the everlasting world perpetually at work" in this world.[32]

For Muir, a recovery of faith was not just a recovery of inner sight. It was also a recovery of compassion and a belief in the interrelatedness of life. As he writes in his diary, "If we could see every human being as an immortal spirit," it would change the way we live and relate.[33] After his Lord's Prayer experience in 1939, he was struck by the importance of the words *we* and *us* in the prayer and the absence of *I* and *me*. It is "collective", he writes. All societies, and the whole of humanity and Earth, form one great family. It is not "*My* Father which art in heaven." It is "*Our* Father which art in heaven." It is not "Give *me* this day my daily bread." It is "Give *us* this day our daily bread." Nor is it "Forgive *my* debts" or "Lead *me* not into temptation" but "Forgive *our* debts" and "Lead *us* not into temptation." Always it is *we* and *us*, and always it holds radical implications for how we are to see and think and live together in interrelationship. To pray "we", he says, is a pledge to all human beings. It is "an act of union" with all that is and "an act of responsibility" for all.[34]

In his poem "The Annunciation", in which he announces a vision of hope for the world, he writes:

> I sing the liberty
> Where each asks from each
> What each most wants to give
> And each awakes in each
> What else would never be
>
> . . .
>
> To make us each for each
> And in our spirit whole.[35]

We are made for one another not only as human beings, he says. We are made to be in relationship with Earth and every life-form. And, thus, he writes in his poem entitled "All We":

> We gave and took the ring
> And pledged ourselves to the earth.[36]

Faith is about faithfulness to the whole human family and to the community of Earth. It is about union with every creature and every human being.

✳

The last decade of Muir's life was one of public recognition and many new opportunities. The "luminous simplicity" of his poetry, as one commentator described it, allowed him to speak deeply into the human soul.[37] Or, perhaps to put it more exactly, it allowed him to speak deeply from *within* the human soul. The British poet and scholar Kathleen Raine said that her encounter with Muir's poetry was not so much an experience of reading his poems as "reliving them".[38] It was almost like hearing his words spoken from deep within her own soul.

The young man who at the age of fourteen had been forced to discontinue his formal education was now being honoured throughout the Western world as a great poet. In 1947 he received honorary doctorates from the Universities of Prague and Edinburgh. In 1955 and 1958, respectively, he was appointed Visiting Professor of English at Harvard University in the United States and then Bristol University in England. Willa too, although not receiving academic appointments like Edwin, was publicly recognized for the excellence of her translation work and for making Kafka's writings widely accessible to the English-speaking world. Between 1946 and 1949 Muir was the director of the British Council in Prague and, after that, in Rome. And, perhaps dearest to him of all, and most challenging, was his appointment to the Wardenship of Newbattle Abbey College in Scotland, established for the higher education of young Scottish men who had been denied the opportunity of completing their basic education at school. This enabled him to guide others on a path he himself had known.

Muir finished his autobiography by saying, "As I look back on the part of the mystery which is my own life … what I am most aware of is that we receive more than we ever give; we receive it from the past, on which we draw with every breath, but also – and this is a point of faith – from the Source of the mystery itself, by means which religious people call Grace."[39]

Muir died on January 3, 1959, in Cambridge and was buried in Swaffham Prior. On his tombstone were inscribed the closing words of his poem "Milton":

> ... His unblinded eyes
> Saw far and near the fields of Paradise.[40]

Faith led Muir to be looking for the light of the eternal in all things and to be experiencing the presence of the immortal within everything that has being. It was a faith that found Christian expression in him and allowed him to stand in an ancient stream of wisdom that fed his soul and deepened his commitment to Earth and humanity. Faith brought him home after years of doubt, to his own true depths and to the source of the mystery that he had experienced on the first day of his life, in a beam of sunlight shining into his cradle. Pure grace!

MEDITATIVE PRACTICE: SEEKING FAITH

Edwin Muir is a messenger of faith to us, not faith in statements about God but faith in the light of the divine deep within every human being and life-form. Muir invites us to remember our first experiences of light, glistening in earth, sea, and sky, and in the eyes of those who love us, and to pledge ourselves in faith to every human being and to the healing of Earth as our shared home.

(pause to listen for what Muir's wisdom stirs in us)

As the doubting heart longs to trust again
so my soul longs for faith
belief in the everlasting world deep in this world
trust in the sacred root that springs still from Eden
and love for the immortal light in all life
waiting forever to rise afresh in us.

(pause to be aware)

As the doubting heart longs to trust again
so my soul longs for faith.

Conclusion

When I first told one of my brothers-in-law about the vision of this book and the nine prophetic figures from whom I would be drawing, he said it sounded as if they were like a "cloud of witnesses" (Heb. 12:1). Either that, he added, or a "motley crew". Maybe both descriptions apply.

In that the great teachers I have focused on in this book come from a variety of backgrounds – different religions, different professions, and different ages – they could at first seem just a motley crew. Is there anything that connects them all? A fair enough question to begin with. But, as we have studied them more closely, we will have discovered that the teachings of these figures derive from a shared love of Earth and the human soul, and a belief that this is where our healing and true sense of home will be found.

When Thomas Berry invites us into a vision of the interrelated universe, he does so by drawing on what he calls the sacred text of Earth and the sacred text of the human soul. Or when Nan Shepherd describes her relationship with the mountain as a love affair, she says that our journey of wonder into the landscape of the natural world is, at the same time, a pilgrimage into the inner landscape of the soul. And when Martin Buber points to the I-Thou relationship at the heart of life, he is calling us to be alert to the divine in every human encounter and every life-form.

Similarly, in Part 2 of the book, when Carl Jung says that awareness is essential in our journey into wholeness, he sees that awareness of the human psyche and awareness of the soul of Earth, or the *anima mundi*, as he calls it, are fundamentally one. Or when Julian of Norwich experiences her revelations of divine love, she sees that nature is of

God just as humanity is of God. And when Jalaluddin Rumi opens the door to love-madness, he is saying that when we adore the beauty of the moon in the night skies, we can be worshipping it also in the inner universe of the soul.

Then, in Part 3 of the book, when Rabindranath Tagore says it is wisdom that leads us into the spiritual world at the heart of this world, he is meaning the spiritual world of the soul as well as the spiritual world of nature. Or when Etty Hillesum invites us to look for meaning and beauty in life even amid terrible suffering, she is inspiring us to pay attention to the yellow jasmine blossoming outside our window, for instance, as well as to its fragrance in the garden of our soul. And, finally, when Edwin Muir creatively reimagines what faith is, he is challenging us to be faithful to the immortal light that shines in every human being and that glistens in earth, sea and sky.

So, what holds this apparently motley crew together is their twin-love of Earth and the human soul. It is this that makes them "a cloud of witnesses" for us today. Not of course that they are the only ones who can guide us in our quest for healing and home. They are, however, a very fine representation of searchers from the past who can help point us in the right direction now. While the teachings of these great prophetic figures were considered in their own day to be out on the edge of religious orthodoxy, today their teachings can be viewed as expressing the very heart of the spiritual quest of this moment in time. And for me, in the writing of this book, these teachers have illuminated the groundwork of my vision and faith.

Also, deep within the shared vision of these nine teachers is a belief in love, whether that be love of Earth and humanity or love as the source of wellness and meaning in our lives. Not only do these great teachers believe in love, they equate love with God. They are all saying, in their wonderfully varied ways, that God is love.

I am completing the writing of this book on the island of Patmos in the Aegean. This is where I wrote my first book thirty-two years ago, and it is a place to which I have returned over the years to be renewed. Legend has it that John the Beloved was here. "God is love," as we have heard him saying, "and those who abide in love abide in God, and God abides in them" (1 John 4:16). Legend also attributes to John the apocalyptic Book of Revelation with its fierce denunciation of the wrongs and injustices of empire which John sees as a seven-headed dragon that will eventually be slain by the sword of truth. Most biblical scholars argue that these writings do not in fact belong to the same person. In other words, there is more than one John in the writings of Christian scripture. I agree. Stylistically they are very different. And they are immensely different in tone and spirit. But it is worth paying attention to what legend has tried to hold together. For love has two distinct expressions. One is a deep "yes" spoken to the sacred essence of Earth and every human being. And the other is an emphatic "no" addressed to anything that violates this sacredness.

So, to speak of Earth and the human soul as sacred, as the great teachers I have cited in this book do, is to be alert to both the "yes" and the "no" of love. The challenge is to live a faithful combination of the two, on the one hand bearing witness to the sacred essence of humanity and Earth, and on the other opposing anything that threatens this sacredness, whether that be ecological, political or religious.

The great nineteenth-century Russian writer Leo Tolstoy, who could well have been included in this book's cloud of witnesses, was passionate about saying "yes" to the true depths of every man and woman and at the same time "no" to the excessive power and privilege of established religion in his homeland. He saw that religion, like everything that comes into being, is born and lives and dies. And after it dies, there is the possibility of it being reborn in ways that may exceed what we have even imagined to be possible. Religion dies, he says, when it forgets the essential vision of its birth. In the case of Christianity, this vision is love, a love for everyone equally, not a love especially for the Tsar of Russia, for example, or for one's own nation over other nations.

Furthermore, love calls us to deeply respect not just the religious leadership and privileged elite of society, but every human being, and especially those who are powerless in our nations, and the life-forms of Earth that have been denied the right of safety and protection.

Religion, as we have known it in the Western world, is dying. We are in a time of transition, not only religiously but politically and ecologically. What is the spiritual vision at the heart of our religious inheritance that we have forgotten or neglected? The Spirit is urging us to remember that we are to do to others, including Earth and every species, what we would most want done unto ourselves. This is the teaching of Jesus at the heart of our Christian inheritance, with its equivalent in the Golden Rule of nearly every great spiritual tradition in the world. And this is the teaching that will guide us into new beginnings.

In our Great Search of today, we are searching for what will bring healing, not only for ourselves, whether as individuals or nations or races, but for all people and for every species. And it is for all things that we are seeking a deeper sense of home address, both physically and spiritually. We are longing for a truer sense of shared origin and spiritual kinship with everything that has being, including a sense of family responsibility for one another. The vision of love at the heart of our religious inheritance can inspire us in our searching, but our searching must never be confined by the boundaries and limitations of our religion.

During this time of transition, many of us, as we have been emphasizing, are in religious exile, whether that be literally as fugitives from our religious tradition or simply as dissatisfied members of it, longing for more depth and vision. The modern Scottish poet Kenneth White says that "exile is the mark of any deep and far-going creativity".[1] By this he means that leaving home, whether that be the home territory of our nation or race or religion, either willingly or by force, presents us with the possibility of expanding our vision beyond what it has been. His emphasis is not on what we are losing in exile, which may be painful and challenging, but on what we are being invited to open to in exile in new and creative ways. And those who are in exile, he adds, will often take with them into exile more of the essential vision of home than what is prevalent in the places they have left. Exile, in its vulnerability and uncertainty, can also be a time of greater openness to new vision and creativity.

This time of spiritual exile in the Western world is a moment in which we are being invited to find relationship with Earth and one another in ways that surpass anything we have known. It is a time of opening to the Spirit in our own depths and the depths of every human being and life-form. And it can be a time of liberation from the closed boundaries of nationhood or race or religion that have confined us in the past and separated us from one another.

We are being invited to remember what we, at some level, have always known, which is that our true spiritual centre is not Rome, for instance, or Jerusalem or Mecca or any of the other places that religion has claimed to hold special authority over us. Our true spiritual centre is Earth and the human soul. Outward places of religious authority and significance may have played an important role in our faith traditions over the centuries but, essentially, they exist to serve Earth and the human soul, not the other way round. The source of truth is deep within each one of us and deep within everything that has being. Just as new science enables us to know that physically we live in an omnicentric universe, so it is spiritually. The centre is everywhere. Our cherished places of religious authority from the past, including our local churches or temples or mosques, can serve us in this moment of transition but only if they remember that the centre of the divine is everywhere, deep in my soul and your soul, and deep in Earth's soul. As Jung said, quoting an ancient hermetic source, "God is a circle whose centre is everywhere and whose circumference is nowhere."[2]

Recently I visited an inter-spiritual community called All Souls Interfaith Gathering in Shelburne, Vermont. We gathered on a Sunday evening in their beautiful sanctuary looking out over the grandeur of Lake Champlain with the peaks of the Adirondack Mountains beyond, accompanied by a combination of mighty thunder and flashes of lightning crashing around us, then shafts of light piercing the black clouds that hung low over the waters. All Souls is a community committed to listening to the Spirit in the body of Earth, in its wildness and beauty, as well as its pain and suffering. And it is a community committed to listening to the Spirit in the human soul, in its struggles and yearnings, as well as its wisdom and imagination.

One of the things that struck me as I spoke to the full sanctuary of men and women who had gathered for the presentation that evening in Vermont, was their range of ethnicities and religious attire. There were Muslim hijabs and Jewish kippahs amid more typical Western clothing as well as the white robes and turbans of Sikhism. At first, they seemed like a motley crew. But the longer I was with them, and the deeper we moved in conversation, the more I realized they were like a modern cloud of witnesses. What they conveyed to me that evening, in spirit and word, was their passion for Earth and the human soul, and their attentiveness to what the Spirit is beckoning us to be and do at this moment in time.

We, of course, don't all have to pursue the path of interfaith gatherings. In fact, it is important that some of us remain firmly rooted in our home traditions so that we can continue to access the unique expressions of wisdom from our respective communities of faith for the blessing of humanity and Earth today. But whether our path takes us into interfaith gatherings or deeply into the faith communities of our origins, we are all needed in this time of transition, as are those who follow a more solitary path of spirituality in this time of exile. Whichever path we choose, we are being urged by the Spirit to turn to Earth and the human soul to listen for inner wisdom to guide us on the path ahead.

We are longing for an expanded vision of the universe, a reawakened love affair with Earth, and a deepened sense of spiritual presence in every moment and encounter of life. We are yearning to grow in awareness, to find wellness in relation to the whole, and to delight in love together. And we are longing for the recovery of wisdom, for meaning in both the joys and the sorrows of life, and for a reimagined faith in the immortal light that shines in all things. These are the yearnings of the Great Search today. If we are true to them, we will be blessed with the graces of healing, both individually and collectively, and we will be graced too with a new sense of home spiritually in our relationship with Earth and one another. It is this that will bless us and our planet in our shared journey toward wholeness. And it is this that will bless those still to be born, our children and our children's children. This is the Great Search that we are invited to be part of, turning to Earth and soul in the quest for healing and home.

Appendix

A Nine-Day Cycle of Meditative Practice

DAY ONE: SEEKING VISION

Thomas Berry is a messenger of vision to us. He invites us to see everything in the universe as both physical and spiritual, and to see that we all began 13.7 billion years ago in the great flaring forth of light. This is our shared story. Will we learn to live it together with the other species of Earth? Or will we continue to pretend that there are two stories, one for humanity and one for the rest of the planet, thus endangering both? It is together that we will flourish.

(pause to listen for what Berry's wisdom stirs in us)

> As the darkness of early morning longs for light
> so my soul longs to see again
> the great spiritual fire of life's beginnings
> still shining
> in galaxies beyond numbering
> and here in me and every lifeform
> countless streams of glory in a single flow of light
> each one irreplaceable.

(pause to be aware)

As the darkness of early morning longs for light
so my soul longs to see again.

DAY TWO: SEEKING EARTH

Nan Shepherd is a messenger to us of oneness with Earth. She invites us to know not just with our minds but with our bodies – to breathe in Earth's freshness, to listen to its silence and storms, to taste its juice in the crispness of an autumn apple, to see its colour in the new light of dawn and feel its wetness in the rain-washed landscape of grasses and trees around us. And in all of this to grow in passion for Earth as a lover for her beloved.

> *(pause to listen for what Shepherd's wisdom stirs in us)*

> As the body longs to waken to all its senses
> so my soul longs to know Earth again
> to breathe her in and touch her
> to taste her goodness and hear her song
> and forever to see fresh shinings of her life
> and seek her healing as my own.

> *(pause to be aware)*

> As the body longs to waken to all its senses
> so my soul longs to know Earth again.

DAY THREE: SEEKING PRESENCE

Martin Buber is a messenger of presence to us. He invites us to be alive to God in one another and in every manifestation of life, and to know that now is the time of divine presence, always now – within us, around us, and between us – and to open our hearts to each moment, looking always for the gift of presence that calls us back to our true selves.

(pause to listen for what Buber's wisdom stirs in us)

> As thirst longs to be quenched
> so my soul longs to drink again
> at the fount of eternal presence
> everywhere
> rising from the wellspring of life
> gracing the countenance of a stranger
> deep in the soil of Earth
> and growing from the ground like a bush on fire.

(pause to be aware)

> As thirst longs to be quenched
> so my soul longs to drink again
> at the fount of eternal presence
> everywhere.

DAY FOUR: SEEKING AWARENESS

Carl Jung is a messenger of awareness to us. He invites us to be alert with love to the light and the shadow, the good and the evil, the beginnings and endings of life that are within us, and to remember the Valley of Diamonds through which we have all travelled in our journey of birth into this world. We come from light, and it is our longing for light that will save us.

(pause to listen for what Jung's wisdom stirs in us)

As morning mist scatters from among the hills
so my soul longs to see again
both light and dark
both height and depth
the one and the many
my life and every life
intertwined
and each a unique manifestation of the divine.

(pause to be aware)

As morning mist scatters from among the hills
so my soul longs to see again.

DAY FIVE: SEEKING WELLNESS

Julian of Norwich is a messenger of wellness to us. She invites us to seek it now and to know that the wellness of the part and the wellness of the whole belong inseparably together. She calls us to look suffering in the face, to feel it and name it, and to ground our hope for healing in the love-longings of the Spirit deep within us, love for those we cherish, love for Earth, love for all. For it is together that we shall be well.

(pause to listen for what Julian's wisdom stirs in us)

As a wounded creature longs for healing
so my soul longs to be well
and for all to be well
healing for Earth
justice for the creatures
and peace for the human family
that we may live together on Earth the promise of Heaven.

(pause to be aware)

As a wounded creature longs for healing
so my soul longs to be well.

DAY SIX: SEEKING LOVE

Jalaluddin Rumi is a messenger of love to us. He invites us to rediscover it as the true essence of religion, and to rebuild our world as a sanctuary of love in which to honour each other and find delight together. When the grape skin of our ego breaks, the rich wine of love flows in us again for Earth and one another.

> *(pause to listen for what Rumi's wisdom stirs in us)*

> As a lover longs for the presence of her beloved
> so my soul longs for the body of Earth
> and the beauty of the human spirit
> that in thought and word and deed each day
> in the costly name of love
> we may live and move as one again
> in the place where the two worlds touch.

> *(pause to be aware)*

> As a lover longs for the presence of her beloved
> so my soul longs to love.

DAY SEVEN: SEEKING WISDOM

Rabindranath Tagore is a messenger of wisdom to us. He invites us to let the wisdom that was knitted into us in our mother's womb come forth again in ever-fresh ways, that we may see the infinite world deep in this world and the eternal Soul in every soul. He calls us to free ourselves from the limitations of self and nation, of religion and race, that we may join the one song, the world-song that is deep in the human soul and the soul of Earth.

(pause to listen for what Tagore's wisdom stirs in us)

As truth longs to be known
so my soul longs for wisdom
that I may see the Sun behind all suns
the Eternal Light in every life
and be a dreamer of dreams for this world
a singer of love's song
everlasting and ever new.

(pause to be aware)

As truth longs to be known
so my soul longs for wisdom.

DAY EIGHT: SEEKING MEANING

Etty Hillesum is a messenger of meaning to us. She invites us to live and breathe through our souls to access the meaning of life in both its glory and agony. She inspires us to defend the dwelling place of the divine deep within us and all life, and to know in our hearts the strength of love to bear all things, hope all things, and endure all things.

(pause to listen for what Hillesum's wisdom stirs in us)

As the mind longs to understand
so my soul yearns for meaning
in both the beauty and pain of life
in the yellow blossoming of jasmine at my window
and its scent in the garden of my soul
in the fears of those who call out at night
and their dread of the journey ahead.
May I find the strength to endure
and witness to the coming of a new day.

(pause to be aware)

As the mind longs to understand
so my soul yearns for meaning.

DAY NINE: SEEKING FAITH

Edwin Muir is a messenger of faith to us, not faith in statements about God but faith in the light of the divine deep within every human being and life-form. Muir invites us to remember our first experiences of light, glistening in earth, sea and sky, and in the eyes of those who love us, and to pledge ourselves in faith to every human being and to the healing of Earth as our shared home.

> *(pause to listen for what Muir's wisdom stirs in us)*

> As the doubting heart longs to trust again
> so my soul longs for faith
> belief in the everlasting world deep in this world
> trust in the sacred root that springs still from Eden
> and love for the immortal light in all life
> waiting forever to rise afresh in us.

> *(pause to be aware)*

> As the doubting heart longs to trust again
> so my soul longs for faith.

Acknowledgments

My children (Rowan, Brendan, Kirsten, and Cameron), for keeping me alert to what so many in their generation are searching for spiritually.

My grandchildren (Ember, Santino, and Lena), for inspiring me to work for the healing of the world they are inheriting.

My wife, Ali, for living and breathing with me over these past few years the wisdom of these nine great teachers.

My colleague Cami Twilling, for setting me free to focus on my writing and teaching.

My literary agent, Roger Freet, for being patient with me when I go through a thousand titles in search of the right one, and so much more.

My former editor at HarperOne, Mickey Maudlin, for wrestling with me to clarify the initial focus of this book.

My editor at HarperOne, Gabriella Page-Fort, for becoming a touchstone of vision in this shared work and granting me extra time to fully grieve the death of my sister, dear Japhia.

Faber & Faber, London, for permission to use Edwin Muir's poems "The Annunciation", "Confirmation", and "Day and Night" from his *Collected Poems* (1984).

And Galileo Publishers, Cambridge, for permission to use Nan Shepherd's poem "Achiltibuie" from *Wild Geese: A Collection of Nan Shepherd's Writings* (2018).

Notes

Introduction

1. Simone Weil, *An Anthology* (London: Penguin, 2005), 150.
2. See John Philip Newell, *Sacred Earth, Sacred Soul* (San Francisco: HarperOne, 2021).
3. Maurice Friedman, *Encounter on the Narrow Ridge: A Life of Martin Buber* (New York: Paragon House, 1993), 329.

Chapter 1. Seeking Vision: Thomas Berry

1. "Morningside Cathedral", *Thomas Berry and the Great Work*, https:// thomasberry.org/morningside-cathedral/.
2. Heather Eaton, ed., *The Intellectual Journey of Thomas Berry: Imagining the Earth Community* (New York: Lexington Books, 2014), vii-viii.
3. Thomas Berry, *The Christian Future and the Fate of Earth* (New York: Orbis Books, 2009), 12.
4. Berry, *The Christian Future and the Fate of Earth*, 60.
5. Thomas Berry, *The Dream of the Earth* (San Francisco: Sierra Club Books, 1988), 132.
6. Thomas Berry, *The Sacred Universe* (New York: Columbia University Press, 2009), 95.
7. Berry, *The Sacred Universe*, 48.
8. Berry, *The Sacred Universe*, 132.
9. Thomas Berry, *The Great Work* (New York: Bell Tower, 1999), 82.
10. "Berry's Call for Engagement of the World Religions", *Thomas Berry and the Great Work*, https://thomasberry.org/life-and-thought/about-thomas-berry/ berrys-call-for-an-awakening-and-exodus/.
11. Berry, *The Sacred Universe*, 78.
12. Berry, *The Sacred Universe*, 78.

13. "Historian of World Religions", *Thomas Berry and the Great Work*, https:// thomasberry.org/life-and-thought/about-thomas-berry/historian-of-world-religions/.
14. Berry, *The Sacred Universe*, 105.
15. Berry, *The Great Work*, 82.16. Muskeke Iskwew, "Grandmother's Creation Story," Indigenous People, https:// www.indigenous-people.net/whitwolf.htm.
17. Eaton, ed., *The Intellectual Journey of Thomas Berry*, vii-viii.
18. Thomas Berry, "The New Story: Comments on the Origin, Identification and Transmission of Values", *Teilhard Studies* 1 (Winter 1978).
19. Berry, *The Christian Future and the Fate of Earth*, 38.
20. Eaton, ed., *The Intellectual Journey of Thomas Berry*, 12.
21. David Bohm, *Wholeness and the Implicate Order* (London: Routledge, 1980), 11.
22. Berry, *The Great Work*, 201.
23. Berry, *The Christian Future and the Fate of Earth*, 63.
24. Berry quoting Cambridge University biologist Norman Myers in *The Great Work*, 164.
25. Berry, *The Sacred Universe*, 138.
26. Berry, *The Christian Future and the Fate of Earth*, 35.
27. Berry quoting Francis Bacon in *The Sacred Universe*, 153.
28. Pierre Teilhard de Chardin, *The Phenomenon of Man* (London: Collins, 1982), 35.
29. Berry, *The Great Work*, 148.
30. Berry, *The Sacred Universe*, 99.
31. Berry, *The Great Work*, 196.
32. Berry, *The Great Work*, 201.
33. Berry, *The Christian Future and the Fate of Earth*, 53.
34. "Morningside Cathedral", *Thomas Berry and the Great Work*, https:// thomasberry.org/morningside-cathedral/.

Chapter 2. Seeking Earth: Nan Shepherd
1. Nan Shepherd, *In the Cairngorms* (Cambridge: Galileo, 2020), 28.
2. Nan Shepherd, "The Quarry Wood", *The Grampian Quartet* (Edinburgh: Canongate, 1996), 5.

3. Nan Shepherd, *The Living Mountain* (Edinburgh: Canongate, 2011), xii.
4. Shepherd, *The Living Mountain*, 1.
5. Shepherd, *The Living Mountain*, 6.
6. Shepherd, *The Living Mountain*, 48.
7. Shepherd, *The Living Mountain*, 107–8.
8. Shepherd, *The Living Mountain*, 11.
9. Charlotte Peacock, ed., *Wild Geese: A Collection of Nan Shepherd's Writing* (Cambridge: Galileo, 2018), 70.
10. Shepherd, *The Living Mountain*, 90.
11. Shepherd, *The Living Mountain*, 91.
12. Shepherd, *The Living Mountain*, 91–93.
13. Shepherd, *The Living Mountain*, 105.
14. Shepherd, *The Living Mountain*, xxxi.
15. Shepherd, *The Living Mountain*, xxxi.
16. Shepherd, *The Living Mountain*, 98.
17. Shepherd, *The Living Mountain*, 53.
18. Shepherd, *The Living Mountain*, 96.
19. Shepherd, *The Living Mountain*, 97.
20. Shepherd, *The Living Mountain*, 101.
21. Shepherd, *The Living Mountain*, 23.
22. Peacock, ed., *Wild Geese*, 43.
23. Peacock, ed., *Wild Geese*, 48.
24. Peacock, ed., *Wild Geese*, 41.
25. Shepherd, *The Living Mountain*, 103.
26. Shepherd, *The Living Mountain*, xxviii, 27.
27. Shepherd, *The Living Mountain*, 103.
28. Shepherd, *In the Cairngorms*, 49.
29. Shepherd, *The Living Mountain*, xliii.
30. Shepherd, *The Living Mountain*, 12–13.
31. Shepherd, *The Living Mountain*, x.
32. Shepherd, *The Living Mountain*, 14.
33. Shepherd, *The Living Mountain*, 14.
34. Shepherd, *The Living Mountain*, xxi.
35. Charlotte Peacock, *Into the Mountain: A Life of Nan Shepherd*

208   The Great Search

(Cambridge: Galileo, 2017), 21.
36. Shepherd, *The Living Mountain*, 15.
37. Shepherd, *The Living Mountain*, 105.
38. Shepherd, *The Living Mountain*, 106.
39. Shepherd, *The Living Mountain*, 108.
40. Shepherd, *The Living Mountain*, 106.
41. Shepherd, *The Living Mountain*, 108.
42. Shepherd, *The Living Mountain*, 108.
43. Shepherd, *The Living Mountain*, 1.
44. Shepherd, *The Living Mountain*, 102.
45. Shepherd, *In the Cairngorms*, 8.
46. Shepherd, *The Living Mountain*, 3.
47. Shepherd, *The Living Mountain*, 61.
48. Shepherd, *In the Cairngorms*, 17.
49. Shepherd, "The Weatherhouse", *The Grampian Quartet*, 112.
50. Shepherd, "The Weatherhouse", *The Grampian Quartet*, 176.
51. Shepherd, "A Pass in the Grampians", *The Grampian Quartet*, 112.
52. Shepherd, *The Living Mountain*, 106.
53. Shepherd, *In the Cairngorms*, 7.
54. Shepherd, *The Living Mountain*, xxiii.
55. Shepherd, *The Living Mountain*, 106.
56. Peacock, ed., *Wild Geese*, 94.
57. Shepherd, *In the Cairngorms*, ix.
58. Peacock, ed., *Wild Geese*, 124.
59. Peacock, *Into the Mountain*, 62.
60. Peacock, ed., *Wild Geese*, 96.
61. Peacock, ed., *Wild Geese*, 94.
62. Shepherd, *The Living Mountain*, 106–7.
63. Shepherd, "The Quarry Wood", *The Grampian Quartet*, 208.
64. Peacock, ed., *Wild Geese*, 64.

Chapter 3. Seeking Presence: Martin Buber
1. Martin Buber, *I and Thou*, trans. Ronald Gregor Smith (Edinburgh: T & T Clark, 1970), 108.
2. Martin Buber, *Two Types of Faith*, trans. Norman P. Goldhawk

(Syracuse: Syracuse University Press, 2003), 84.
3. Buber, *I and Thou*, 3.
4. Buber, *I and Thou*, 6.
5. Buber, *I and Thou*, 3.
6. Buber, *I and Thou*, 18.
7. Martin Buber, *Between Man and Man*, trans. Ronald Gregor Smith (Mansfield: Martino Publishing, 2014), 88.
8. Buber, *I and Thou*, 27.
9. Buber, *Between Man and Man*, 23.
10. Buber, *Two Types of Faith*, 158.
11. Maurice Friedman, *Encounter on the Narrow Ridge: A Life of Martin Buber* (New York: Paragon House, 1993), 452.
12. Friedman, *Encounter on the Narrow Ridge*, 348.
13. Friedman, *Encounter on the Narrow Ridge*, 333–34.
14. Buber, *I and Thou*, 115.
15. Buber, *I and Thou*, 114.
16. Buber, *Two Types of Faith*, 26.
17. Buber, *I and Thou*, 98.
18. Friedman, *Encounter on the Narrow Ridge*, 63.
19. Buber, *I and Thou*, 81.
20. Friedman, *Encounter on the Narrow Ridge*, 78.
21. Friedman, *Encounter on the Narrow Ridge*, 192.
22. Friedman, *Encounter on the Narrow Ridge*, 338.
23. Friedman, *Encounter on the Narrow Ridge*, 29.
24. Buber, *I and Thou*, 80.
25. Martin Buber, *Images of Good and Evil*, trans. Michael Bullock (London: Routledge & Kegan Paul, 1952), 39.
26. Buber, *I and Thou*, 46.
27. Buber, *Images of Good and Evil*, 21.
28. Friedman, *Encounter on the Narrow Ridge*, 345.
29. Friedman, *Encounter on the Narrow Ridge*, 215.
30. Friedman, *Encounter on the Narrow Ridge*, 275.
31. Friedman, *Encounter on the Narrow Ridge*, 336.
32. Friedman, *Encounter on the Narrow Ridge*, 336.
33. Maurice Friedman, *Martin Buber: The Life of Dialogue* (London:

Routledge, 2002), 128.
34. Buber, *I and Thou*, 100.
35. Friedman, *Encounter on the Narrow Ridge*, 45.
36. Buber, *I and Thou*, 120.
37. Friedman, *Encounter on the Narrow Ridge*, 388.
38. Buber, *Two Types of Faith*, 158–59.
39. Friedman, *Encounter on the Narrow Ridge*, 256.
40. Buber, *Two Types of Faith*, 12–13.
41. Buber, *Two Types of Faith*, 75.
42. Friedman, *Encounter on the Narrow Ridge*, 293.
43. Friedman, *Encounter on the Narrow Ridge*, 459.
44. Friedman, *Encounter on the Narrow Ridge*, 60.
45. Friedman, *Encounter on the Narrow Ridge*, 458.
46. Friedman, *Encounter on the Narrow Ridge*, 260.
47. Buber, *Between Man and Man*, 83.
48. Buber, *Between Man and Man*, 114.

Chapter 4. Seeking Awareness: Carl Jung
1. C. G. Jung, *The Archetypes and the Collective Unconscious: The Collected Works of C. G. Jung*, vol. 9, part 1, trans. R. F. C. Hull (London: Routledge, 1990), 253.
2. C. G. Jung, *Memories, Dreams, Reflections*, trans. Richard Winston and Clara Winston (New York: Vintage, 1989), 269.
3. Jung, *Memories, Dreams, Reflections*, v.
4. Jung, *Memories, Dreams, Reflections*, 104.
5. Jung, *Memories, Dreams, Reflections*, 358.
6. Jung, *The Archetypes and the Collective Unconscious*, 211.
7. C. G. Jung, *Psychology and Religion: The Collected Works of C. G. Jung*, vol. 11, trans. R. F. C. Hull (Princeton: Princeton University Press, 1975), 17.
8. C. G. Jung, *Mysterium Coniunctionis: The Collected Works of C. G. Jung*, vol. 14, trans. R. F. C. Hull (Princeton: Princeton University Press, 1989), 478.
9. Jung, *Memories, Dreams, Reflections*, xi.
10. Jung, *Memories, Dreams, Reflections*, 4.

11. Jung, *The Archetypes and the Collective Unconscious*, 8.
12. C. G. Jung, *Aion: The Collected Works of C. G. Jung*, vol 9, part 2, trans. R. F. C. Hull (Princeton: Princeton University Press, 1979), 178.
13. Jung, *Memories, Dreams, Reflections*, 141.
14. See Rudolf Otto, *The Idea of the Holy*, trans. John W. Harvey (London: Oxford University Press, 1923).
15. See Friedrich Nietzsche, *The Gay Science*, trans. Walter Kaufmann (New York: Vintage, 1974).
16. Jung, *Psychology and Religion*, 90.
17. Jung, *Psychology and Religion*, 50.
18. Jung, *Memories, Dreams, Reflections*, 39.
19. Jung, *Memories, Dreams, Reflections*, 40.
20. Jung, *Memories, Dreams, Reflections*, 48.
21. Jung, *Memories, Dreams, Reflections*, 50.
22. C. G. Jung, *Aspects of the Feminine*, trans. R. F. C. Hull (London: Ark, 1992), 72.
23. Jung, *Memories, Dreams, Reflections*, 158–59.
24. Jung, *Mysterium Coniunctionis*, 180.
25. Jung, *Psychology and Religion*, 42.
26. Jung, *Memories, Dreams, Reflections*, 134.
27. Jung, *Memories, Dreams, Reflections*, 175.
28. Jung, *Aion*, 87.
29. Jung, *Aion*, 166.
30. Jung, *Memories, Dreams, Reflections*, 193.
31. Jung, *Aion*, 268.
32. Jung, *Aspects of the Feminine*, 44.
33. Jung, *Mysterium Coniunctionis*, 428.
34. Jung, *Mysterium Coniunctionis*, 364.
35. Jung, *Psychology and Religion*, 180.
36. Jung, *Aion*, 86.
37. Jung, *Aion*, 164.
38. Jung, *Aion*, 143.
39. Jung, *Psychology and Religion*, 89.
40. Jung, *Memories, Dreams, Reflections*, 210–11.

41. Jung, *Memories, Dreams, Reflections*, 354.
42. Jung, *Memories, Dreams, Reflections*, 331.
43. Jung, *Psychology and Religion*, 89.
44. Jung, *The Archetypes and the Collective Unconscious*, 160.
45. Jung, *The Archetypes and the Collective Unconscious*, 164.
46. Jung, *Memories, Dreams, Reflections*, 358.
47. Jung, *Memories, Dreams, Reflections*, 359.

Chapter 5. Seeking Wellness: Julian of Norwich
1. Julian of Norwich, *Revelations of Divine Love*, trans. Elizabeth Spearing (London: Penguin, 1998), 80.
2. Julian of Norwich, *Revelations of Divine Love*, 10.
3. Julian of Norwich, *Revelations of Divine Love*, 58.
4. Julian of Norwich, *Showings*, trans. Edmund Colledge and James Walsh (Mahwah, NJ: Paulist Press, 1978), 290.
5. Julian of Norwich, *Revelations of Divine Love*, 160.
6. Julian of Norwich, *Revelations of Divine Love*, 129.
7. Julian of Norwich, *Revelations of Divine Love*, 130.
8. Julian of Norwich, *Revelations of Divine Love*, 132.
9. Julian of Norwich, *Revelations of Divine Love*, 133.
10. Julian of Norwich, *Revelations of Divine Love*, 153.
11. Julian of Norwich, *Revelations of Divine Love*, 134.
12. Julian of Norwich, *Revelations of Divine Love*, 129.
13. Julian of Norwich, *Revelations of Divine Love*, 125.
14. Julian of Norwich, *Revelations of Divine Love*, 148–49.
15. Julian of Norwich, *Revelations of Divine Love*, 12.
16. Julian of Norwich, *Revelations of Divine Love*, 118–19.
17. Julian of Norwich, *Revelations of Divine Love*, 21.
18. Julian of Norwich, *Revelations of Divine Love*, 35.
19. Julian of Norwich, *Revelations of Divine Love*, 146.
20. Julian of Norwich, *Revelations of Divine Love*, 169.
21. Julian of Norwich, *Revelations of Divine Love*, 170.
22. Julian of Norwich, *Revelations of Divine Love*, 166.
23. Julian of Norwich, *Revelations of Divine Love*, 166.
24. Julian of Norwich, *Revelations of Divine Love*, 146.

25. Julian of Norwich, *Revelations of Divine Love*, 175.
26. Julian of Norwich, *Revelations of Divine Love*, 146.
27. Julian of Norwich, *Revelations of Divine Love*, 26.
28. Julian of Norwich, *Revelations of Divine Love*, 26.
29. Julian of Norwich, *Revelations of Divine Love*, 7.
30. Julian of Norwich, *Revelations of Divine Love*, 89.
31. Julian of Norwich, *Revelations of Divine Love*, 25.
32. Philip Ziegler, *The Black Death* (London: Faber & Faber, 2008), 128.
33. Julian of Norwich, *Revelations of Divine Love*, 139.
34. Julian of Norwich, *Revelations of Divine Love*, 179.
35. Julian of Norwich, *Revelations of Divine Love*, 105.
36. Julian of Norwich, *Revelations of Divine Love*, 85–86.
37. Julian of Norwich, *Revelations of Divine Love*, 139.
38. Julian of Norwich, *Revelations of Divine Love*, 30.
39. Julian of Norwich, *Revelations of Divine Love*, 147.
40. Julian of Norwich, *Revelations of Divine Love*, 103.
41. Julian of Norwich, *Revelations of Divine Love*, 20.
42. Julian of Norwich, *Revelations of Divine Love*, 162.
43. Julian of Norwich, *Revelations of Divine Love*, 104.
44. Julian of Norwich, *Revelations of Divine Love*, 27.
45. Julian of Norwich, *Revelations of Divine Love*, 113.
46. Julian of Norwich, *Revelations of Divine Love*, 10.
47. Julian of Norwich, *Revelations of Divine Love*, 34.
48. Julian of Norwich, *Revelations of Divine Love*, 179.
49. T. S. Eliot, *Collected Poems* (London: Faber & Faber, 1963), 222–23.

Chapter 6. Seeking Love: Jalaluddin Rumi

1. Jalaluddin Rumi, *Selected Poems*, trans. C. Banks (London: Penguin, 1995), 10.
2. Rumi, *Selected Poems*, 17–18.
3. Rumi, *Selected Poems*, 18.
4. Rumi, *Selected Poems*, 103.
5. Rumi, *Selected Poems*, 229.

6. Rumi, *Selected Poems*, 9.
7. Franklin Lewis, *Rumi: Past and Present, East and West* (Oxford: Oneworld, 2001), 200.
8. Rumi, *Selected Poems*, 229.
9. Rumi, *Selected Poems*, 41.
10. Rumi, *Selected Poems*, 166–67.
11. Rumi, *Selected Poems*, 36.
12. Rumi, *Selected Poems*, 32.
13. See Barbara Brown Taylor, *Holy Envy: Finding God in the Faith of Others* (San Francisco: HarperOne, 2018).
14. Rumi, *Selected Poems*, 22.
15. Rumi, *Selected Poems*, 94.
16. Rumi, *Selected Poems*, 13.
17. Rumi, *Selected Poems*, 189.
18. Rumi, *Selected Poems*, 255.
19. Rumi, *Selected Poems*, 101.
20. Rumi, *Selected Poems*, 34.
21. Rumi, *Selected Poems*, 113.
22. Rumi, *Selected Poems*, 239–42.
23. Rumi, *Selected Poems*, 34.
24. Rumi, *Selected Poems*, 278–79.
25. Lewis, *Rumi*, 408.
26. Rumi, *Selected Poems*, 246.
27. Jalaluddin Rumi, "One Song" (trans. Coleman Banks), https://www.uri.org/uri-story/20210310-one-song-rumi.
28. Rumi, *Selected Poems*, 40.
29. Rumi, *Selected Poems*, 6.
30. Rumi, *Selected Poems*, 201–2.
31. Rumi, *Selected Poems*, 37.
32. Jalaluddin Rumi, "The Body is like Mary" (trans. Daniel Ladinsky), https://sufispirit.com.au/feature/rumi-sufi-poetry-body-like-mary/.
33. Rumi, *Selected Poems*, 243.
34. Rumi, *Selected Poems*, 87.
35. Rumi, *Selected Poems*, 1.
36. Rumi, *Selected Poems*, 22.

37. Rumi, *Selected Poems*, 14.
38. Rumi, *Selected Poems*, 16.
39. Rumi, *Selected Poems*, 91.
40. Rumi, *Selected Poems*, 193.
41. Rumi, *Selected Poems*, 85–86.
42. Rumi, *Selected Poems*, 180.
43. Rumi, *Selected Poems*, 92.
44. Rumi, *Selected Poems*, 275.
45. Rumi, *Selected Poems*, 207.
46. Rumi, *Selected Poems*, 106.
47. Rumi, *Selected Poems*, 125.
48. Rumi, *Selected Poems*, 77.

Chapter 7. Seeking Wisdom: Rabindranath Tagore

1. Rabindranath Tagore, *My Life in My Words* (New Delhi: Penguin, 2006), 140.
2. Rabindranath Tagore, *The Religion of Man* (Rhinebeck: Monkfish, 2004), 99.
3. Rabindranath Tagore, *Sadhana: The Realisation of Life* (London: Macmillan, 1914), 11.
4. Tagore, *My Life in My Words*, 161.
5. Tagore, *My Life in My Words*, 173.
6. Tagore, *My Life in My Words*, 165.
7. Tagore, *My Life in My Words*, 195.
8. Amiya Chakravarty, ed., *A Tagore Reader* (Boston: Beacon Press, 1961), 38.
9. Tagore, *My Life in My Words*, 181.
10. Tagore, *Sadhana*, 4.
11. Tagore, *The Religion of Man*, 142.
12. Tagore, *Sadhana*, 5.
13. Tagore, *Sadhana*, 12.
14. Tagore, *Sadhana*, 10.
15. Tagore, *My Life in My Words*, 367.
16. Tagore, *The Religion of Man*, 77–78.
17. Tagore, *My Life in My Words*, 96.

18. Tagore, *My Life in My Words*, 28.
19. Tagore, *The Religion of Man*, 70–71.
20. Tagore, *My Life in My Words*, 28.
21. Chakravarty, ed., *A Tagore Reader*, 30–31.
22. Herbert Vetter, ed., *The Heart of God: Prayers of Rabindranath Tagore* (Vermont: Tuttle Publishing, 1997). 6.
23. Tagore, *My Life in My Words*, 83.
24. Vetter, ed., *The Heart of God*, 46.
25. Tagore, *The Religion of Man*, 72.
26. Tagore, *My Life in My Words*, 326.
27. Tagore, *My Life in My Words*, 322.
28. Tagore, *My Life in My Words*, 322.
29. Tagore, *The Religion of Man*, 137.
30. Tagore, *Sadhana*, 37.
31. Tagore, *The Religion of Man*, 45.
32. Rabindranath Tagore, *Gitanjali* (London: Macmillan, 1914), 8–9.
33. Tagore, *My Life in My Words*, 335.
34. Tagore, *Sadhana*, 8.
35. Tagore, *Sadhana*, 36.
36. Tagore, *Gitanjali*, 66.
37. Tagore, *Sadhana*, 17.
38. Tagore, *My Life in My Words*, 139.
39. Tagore, *My Life in My Words*, 330–31.
40. V. Bhatia, ed., "The Parrot's Training", *Rabindranath Tagore: Pioneer in Education* (New Delhi: Sahitya Chayan, 1994).
41. Tagore, *The Religion of Man*, 78.
42. Tagore, *The Religion of Man*, 8.
43. Tagore, *My Life in My Words*, 261.
44. Tagore, *Sadhana*, 28.
45. Tagore, *Sadhana*, 16.
46. Tagore, *The Religion of Man*, 152.
47. Tagore, *Sadhana*, 29.
48. Tagore, *Sadhana*, 77.
49. Tagore, *Sadhana*, 20.
50. Tagore, *My Life in My Words*, 97.

51. Chakravarty, ed., *A Tagore Reader*, 9.
52. Jallianwala Bagh massacre, *Wikipedia*, https://en.wikipedia.org/wiki/Jallianwala_ Bagh_massacre.
53. Jana Gana Mana, *Wikipedia*, https://en.wikipedia.org/wiki/Jana_Gana_Mana.
54. Chakravarty, ed., *A Tagore Reader*, 38.
55. Tagore, *My Life in My Words*, 192.
56. Tagore, *My Life in My Words*, 191.
57. Tagore, *My Life in My Words*, 192.
58. Tagore, *The Religion of Man*, 50.
59. Tagore, *My Life in My Words*, 193.
60. Tagore, *My Life in My Words*, 181.
61. Tagore, *My Life in My Words*, 182.
62. Tagore, *The Religion of Man*, 99.
63. Tagore, *The Religion of Man*, 134–35.
64. Chakravarty, ed., *A Tagore Reader*, 37.
65. Tagore, *Sadhana*, 62.
66. Tagore, *My Life in My Words*, 194.
67. Tagore, *My Life in My Words*, 199.
68. Tagore, *My Life in My Words*, 195.
69. Tagore, *Sadhana*, 70.
70. Tagore, *Sadhana*, 143.
71. Vetter, ed., *The Heart of God*, 9.
72. Vetter, ed., *The Heart of God*, x.
73. Vetter, ed., *The Heart of God*, 75.

Chapter 8. Seeking Meaning: Etty Hillesum
1. Etty Hillesum, *An Interrupted Life: The Diaries and Letters of Etty Hillesum 1941–43*, trans. Arnold J. Pomerans (London: Persephone Books, 1999), 223–24.
2. Hillesum, *An Interrupted Life*, 255–56.
3. Hillesum, *An Interrupted Life*, 19.
4. Hillesum, *An Interrupted Life*, 199.
5. Hillesum, *An Interrupted Life*, 249.
6. Hillesum, *An Interrupted Life*, 33.

7. Hillesum, *An Interrupted Life*, 53.
8. Hillesum, *An Interrupted Life*, 34.
9. Hillesum, *An Interrupted Life*, 35.
10. Hillesum, *An Interrupted Life*, 89.
11. Hillesum, *An Interrupted Life*, 90.
12. Hillesum, *An Interrupted Life*, 129.
13. Hillesum, *An Interrupted Life*, 90.
14. Hillesum, *An Interrupted Life*, 279.
15. Hillesum, *An Interrupted Life*, 129.
16. Hillesum, *An Interrupted Life*, 33.
17. Hillesum, *An Interrupted Life*, 163.
18. Hillesum, *An Interrupted Life*, 13.
19. Hillesum, *An Interrupted Life*, 134.
20. Hillesum, *An Interrupted Life*, 116.
21. Hillesum, *An Interrupted Life*, 44.
22. Hillesum, *An Interrupted Life*, 250.
23. Hillesum, *An Interrupted Life*, 57.
24. Hillesum, *An Interrupted Life*, 96.
25. Hillesum, *An Interrupted Life*, 160.
26. Hillesum, *An Interrupted Life*, 182.
27. Hillesum, *An Interrupted Life*, 107.
28. Hillesum, *An Interrupted Life*, 164.
29. Hillesum, *An Interrupted Life*, 118–19.
30. Hillesum, *An Interrupted Life*, 184.
31. Hillesum, *An Interrupted Life*, 185–87.
32. Hillesum, *An Interrupted Life*, 219.
33. Hillesum, *An Interrupted Life*, 217.
34. Hillesum, *An Interrupted Life*, 220.
35. Hillesum, *An Interrupted Life*, 239.
36. Hillesum, *An Interrupted Life*, 162.
37. Hillesum, *An Interrupted Life*, 301.
38. Hillesum, *An Interrupted Life*, 253.
39. Hillesum, *An Interrupted Life*, 274–75.
40. Hillesum, *An Interrupted Life*, 402.
41. Hillesum, *An Interrupted Life*, 408. See also the biblical story of King Herod and the slaughter of the innocents (Matt. 2:16).

42. Hillesum, *An Interrupted Life*, 189.
43. Hillesum, *An Interrupted Life*, 242.
44. Hillesum, *An Interrupted Life*, 218.
45. Hillesum, *An Interrupted Life*, 312.
46. Hillesum, *An Interrupted Life*, 213.
47. Hillesum, *An Interrupted Life*, 277.
48. Hillesum, *An Interrupted Life*, 216.
49. Hillesum, *An Interrupted Life*, 187.
50. Hillesum, *An Interrupted Life*, 50.
51. Hillesum, *An Interrupted Life*, 211–12.
52. Hillesum, *An Interrupted Life*, 274.
53. Hillesum, *An Interrupted Life*, 355.
54. Hillesum, *An Interrupted Life*, 333.
55. Hillesum, *An Interrupted Life*, 267.
56. Hillesum, *An Interrupted Life*, 177.
57. Hillesum, *An Interrupted Life*, 424.
58. Hillesum, *An Interrupted Life*, 282.
59. Hillesum, *An Interrupted Life*, 305.
60. Hillesum, *An Interrupted Life*, 395.
61. Hillesum, *An Interrupted Life*, 227.
62. Hillesum, *An Interrupted Life*, 426.
63. Hillesum, *An Interrupted Life*, 429.

Chapter 9. Seeking Faith: Edwin Muir
1. Edwin Muir, *An Autobiography* (London: Hogarth Press, 1980), 18.
2. Muir, *An Autobiography*, 25.
3. Muir, *An Autobiography*, 27.
4. Muir, *An Autobiography*, 58.
5. Muir, *An Autobiography*, 26.
6. Muir, *An Autobiography*, 28.
7. Muir, *An Autobiography*, 22–23.
8. Edwin Muir, *Collected Poems* (London: Faber & Faber, 1984), 228.
9. Muir, *An Autobiography*, 86–87.
10. Muir, *An Autobiography*, 80.
11. Peter H. Butter, *Edwin Muir: Man and Poet* (Edinburgh: Oliver & Boyd, 1966), 163.

12. Muir, *Collected Poems*, 157.
13. Muir, *An Autobiography*, 91.
14. Muir, *An Autobiography*, 145.
15. Muir, *An Autobiography*, 153–54.
16. Muir, *Collected Poems*, 118.
17. Butter, *Edwin Muir*, 90–91.
18. Muir, *An Autobiography*, 54.
19. Muir, *Collected Poems*, 239.
20. Muir, *An Autobiography*, 33.
21. Muir, *Collected Poems*, 227.
22. Butter, *Edwin Muir*, 287.
23. Muir, *An Autobiography*, 192–93.
24. Butter, *Edwin Muir*, 123.
25. Butter, *Edwin Muir*, 162.
26. Butter, *Edwin Muir*, 156.
27. Muir, *An Autobiography*, 246.
28. Muir, *An Autobiography*, 247.
29. Peter H. Butter, ed., *Selected Letters of Edwin Muir* (London: Hogarth Press, 1974), 118.
30. Butter, ed., *Selected Letters of Edwin Muir*, 115–16.
31. Muir, *Collected Poems*, 134.
32. Muir, *Collected Poems*, 198.
33. Butter, *Edwin Muir*, 161.
34. Butter, *Edwin Muir*, 168.
35. Muir, *Collected Poems*, 117.
36. Muir, *Collected Poems*, 158.
37. Butter, *Edwin Muir*, 188.
38. Butter, ed., *Selected Letters of Edwin Muir*, 7.
39. Muir, *An Autobiography*, 281.
40. Muir, *Collected Poems*, 207.

Conclusion
1. Cairns Craig, ed., *The Collected Works of Kenneth White*, vol. 2 (Edinburgh: Edinburgh University Press, 2021), 186.
2. Jung, *Psychology and Religion*, 155.